Friendship

Friendship

The Forgotten Spiritual Discipline

PAMELA BAKER POWELL

Foreword by Crystal L. Downing

WIPF & STOCK · Eugene, Oregon

FRIENDSHIP
The Forgotten Spiritual Discipline

Wipf & Stock
An Imprint of Wipf and Stock Publishers
199 W. 8th Ave., Suite 3
Eugene, OR 97401

www.wipfandstock.com

PAPERBACK ISBN: 978-1-6667-5036-2
HARDCOVER ISBN: 978-1-6667-5037-9
EBOOK ISBN: 978-1-6667-5038-6

VERSION NUMBER 04/10/24

To cherished friends of my life

Contents

Foreword

IN *THE FOUR LOVES*, C. S. Lewis explores different Greek terms for love—
agape, *eros*, *philia*, and *storge*—discussing how the difference among them
illuminates human relationships. Commissioned by the BBC, Lewis read
his work aloud for several radio broadcasts in 1958, thus providing us with
rare examples of his booming deep voice.

In *Friendship: The Forgotten Spiritual Discipline*, Pamela Powell summarizes the Greek distinctions for love that motivated Lewis: "*Agape*—the
love that God extends to us and the love that through God we extend to
others; *eros*—the love of physical passion and the love of beauty and the
arts; *philia*—the love that we have for our friends; *storge*—the love that is
affection for things and people we like."[1] And though her insights were not
originally broadcast on radio, Pamela's voice rings from every page, drawing readers in through her engagingly descriptive stories of pain and joy in
her own life, using most as either metaphors or illustrations of how friendship works. Doing so, Pamela implies that the important Greek distinctions
for love are subsumed into the category of *philia*, since God's very nature
endorses friendship. Indeed, essential to Christian doctrine is the fact that
God is not unitary; God is inherently relational, the Trinity implying constant communion among Father, Son, and Holy Ghost. And that relational
God, Pamela argues, wants to be in communion with all of creation, especially beings created in God's own image (Gen 1:27).

Pamela's emphasis reminds me of the distinction between Eastern
Orthodox and Western views of the Trinity, as explained by theologian
Catherine Mowry LaCugna. Western Christians tend to think of God as
one "substance" with three beings, to the end that being seems to precede

1. Powell, *Friendship: The Forgotten Spiritual Discipline*, 40.

relationship. In contrast, the Eastern Orthodox Church believes that "communion underlies being," such that "personhood," like that of the God in whose image we are made, suggests "someone toward another."[2] LaCugna thus helped me understand the philosophy of Russian Orthodox Mikhail Bakhtin, who argued that one cannot know oneself without relationship to the other.

Pamela makes the exact same argument as Bakhtin, for a popular rather than scholarly audience. While Bakhtin coins the word *heteroglossia*, to describe, in part, the "different tongues" that make up the self,[3] she practices what Bakhtin theorizes by interweaving other Christian tongues with her own, from family members to friends, from Aristotle to Bonhoeffer, from Gospel writers to Annie Dillard. One voice, however, intersects with Pamela's more than any other: that of an early twelfth-century monk named Aelred, who left behind the relatively luxurious life of the Scottish court by joining a monastery at Rievaulx in Yorkshire, eventually becoming its abbot. Pamela repeatedly quotes from Aelred's book *Spiritual Friendship*, showing how Aelred has influenced her thought, as though endorsing Bakhtin's statement that language is "populated—overpopulated—with the intentions of others."[4]

Reading Pamela's book is like sitting with a group of close friends who, while discussing aspects of friendship, generate heteroglossia by quoting different Bible verses, alluding to different historical figures, or offering different examples one right after another, some quite personal, others more literary. She thus weaves together multiple threads in the loom of *Friendship: The Forgotten Spiritual Discipline* that together look like the underside of a tapestry, with multiple strings and knots hanging down—until one sees the finished product. Pamela's tapestry reminds me of Michelangelo's painting on the ceiling of the Sistine Chapel: Creator God, accompanied by angels, reaches out his finger to a half-reclined Adam. Rather than proclaiming "love is love," the tapestry communicates "communion underlies being."

Significantly, Pamela alludes to the way Tolkien ignited a friendship with C. S. Lewis, reminding me that relationship preceded being for the Inklings, a group of scholars who practiced the dialogism of heteroglossia when they met in their Oxford University rooms as well as local pubs to

2. LaCugna, "God in Communion," 89.

3. Bakhtin, "Discourse in the Novel," 291–92.

4. Bakhtin, "Discourse in the Novel," 294.

discuss not only their writings but also their faith. Friendship, as Pamela defines it, explains the power of the Inklings to change culture, even though members argued with and mocked each other. As often noted by Lewis scholar David C. Downing, "If it had not been for Tolkien, we would never have heard of C. S. Lewis, since Tolkien helped Lewis surmount his resistance to Christian doctrine. And if it had not been for Lewis, we would never have heard of Tolkien, because it was Lewis who kept prodding Tolkien to stop tinkering with his fantasy epics and get them published."[5] Their friendship led to a tapestry that has shown what Christian creation can look like.

Reading *Friendship: The Forgotten Spiritual Discipline* thus reminded me of the important friendship groups I have had in my life: a special group that met in Pasadena, California, where several attended Fuller Seminary (as did Pamela Powell); a special group that met in Santa Barbara, California, to discuss politics, religion, and film; and, in central Pennsylvania, a special group of professors who met for a book club as well as a special group of published women writers called "The Pinklings." And now I live in Chicagoland, co-directing with my husband, David C. Downing, an archive that celebrates the power of friendship: the Marion E. Wade Center, which oversees the most comprehensive collection in the world for published and unpublished materials by and about C. S. Lewis and six of his important influences, like Tolkien: friends who contributed to his heteroglossia, both in the flesh and through the fleshing out of imaginative thoughts in their works.

A statement in *The Four Loves* beautifully communicates Lewis's celebration of *philia*, but also summarizes Pamela's purposes in her book: "Christ, who said to the disciples 'Ye have not chosen me, but I have chosen you,' can truly say to every group of Christian friends, 'You have not chosen one another but I have chosen you for one another.' The Friendship is not a reward for our discrimination and good taste in finding one another out. It is the instrument by which God reveals to each the beauties of all the others."[6] Significantly, throughout his life, Lewis considered his brother Warren (Warnie) one of his best friends, lending great significance to Pamela's chapter on family and friendship. Reading Pamela's insights, I suddenly realized that my best friend in the world, with whom I can share all my thoughts, both uplifting and degrading, is a family member: my

5. David C. Downing, co-director of the Marion E. Wade Center, in lectures and conversations around the country.

6. Lewis, *Four Loves*, 126.

sister-in-law, who manifests the fruits of the Spirit more than anyone else I know. And her sharing with me of those fruit-full gifts draws me closer to Christ, fulfilling the ideal friendship outlined by Pamela.

Blessed by her assessment of how and why friendships live and die, I am grateful that Pamela introduced me to Aelred of Rievaulx, who argues that Christian friendships are eternal. She has convinced me that humans are "hardwired" to be relational, as she puts it, starting with the umbilical cord. How interesting, then, that God used an umbilical cord to enter the world in the flesh, suggesting that communion precedes being not only for the Trinity, but also for the *imago Dei*!

Crystal L. Downing
Co-Director of the Marion E. Wade Center
Wheaton, Illinois

Preface

Maybe you think you know all about friendship. Everybody does, right?

But what if you're missing something very important about friendship, something you have never really considered before? What if friendship has an important spiritual dimension? What if building these friendships is a spiritual practice (or discipline) that deepens your life in Christ and even enriches your eternal life?

That's what this book is about.

I am a pastor by calling and a professor by extension of that calling. Over the course of the years it has taken to pastor four churches and teach on two theological faculties, I have been preaching and teaching what academics call practical theology, what it means to live an authentic Christian life in our daily lives. Christians have been considering this since the first century. There is lots to go on!

Learning about friendship over the ages is a gold mine of wisdom from the ancient Greeks and Romans, to Jesus himself, to Paul, to a Christian monk in the 1100s in Northern England, who wrote the definitive guide to friendship. The marvelous truth is that finding and building friendships is one of the most important topics engaged by thinkers of all stripes. Theologians and philosophers overwhelmingly find that friendship is one of the supreme joys of human life.

Yet a little book written by Aelred of Rievaulx in twelfth-century England continues to be the primer for Christians. Aelred found that friendships in Christ uniquely impact our earthly spiritual formation and prepare us for the joy of the eternal blessing. It is in friendship that many of the sweetest blessings of human life are experienced, not just of earthly life, but heavenly life as well.

We know from Scripture that God intended us to live in meaningful relationships. All people, no matter religious affiliation or nationality or age, are created to be in relationship with others. One could argue that it is a creation ordinance. We all know that true friendships bless our life's journey.

Yet in modern days and teachings, little has been written about friendship as a meaningful aspect of the Christian life, a spiritual discipline.

True, in the past half century there has been a revival of interest in the spiritual disciplines. There has been a wealth of writing and teaching on this rich topic. Yet, a majority of these disciplines focus on what believers can do alone, in private, in their relationship with God. Jesus's words that the most important aspects of a faithful life are to love God and neighbor as oneself are articulated, but loving neighbor is often relegated to charitable expressions.

My question is: What if we're missing something? Something crucial. What if we've missed one of the most important aspects of our life on earth and in eternity?

Significantly, after birth, there is only one human relationship that is available to every human being on earth: friendship.

For Christians that relationship extends to the opportunity to build friendship with other believers who share life together and the love of God with one another. When we are in a relationship like that, we find that we are changed. We find more joy. We find more hope. We realize that we are not living life alone. Our faith deepens. When we are in a relationship like that, we begin to be formed more fully into the person God created us to be. It is in this relationship of Christian friendship that the crucible of spiritual formation takes place.

But that isn't all. There is a life beyond this life, an eternal life. Have you ever thought that the friendships in Christ that you make in this life will continue into eternity? Scripture tells us so.

So, in fact, friendship isn't just a luxury for now. It is a lifeblood for eternity!

When you understand your real friendships as God-sent, your whole relational life changes.

It's transformational. That is why I have written this book.

The question for you is invitational: Will you join me on this journey of exploration of one of the greatest joys and blessings of human life, the journey of Christian friendship?

I am hoping and praying that you will.

Acknowledgments

No book is ever written alone.
I want to thank members of my family, all wordsmiths:
My husband: John Paul Powell
My daughter: Jennifer Powell McNutt
My son-in-law: David W. McNutt
My two sons: Stewart Jefferson Powell
Elliott Jefferson Powell
My life-long friends with whom I learned the joy and the blessing of friendship:
Karen Womer Berns
Marcia Burkert Belt
My dear professor friends, Glen and Kate Scorgie
My first small group at Tabernacle Church, Indianapolis, IN
My National Covenant Group of clergy
The Women of the First Presbyterian Church of Glen Ellyn, IL
Cinda Siligmueller, the Director of Adult Ministries
The Women of the Faith Builders Bible Study
who faithfully listened to each new chapter as it was written
And finally, the cherished friends who emerged from the churches I pastored,
as well as the seminaries where I taught.
You are dear to me. You know who you are.

I gratefully acknowledge all of you, for you are a big part of the pages that follow here.

1

Friendship
The Eternal Spiritual Blessing

I THINK ABOUT HEAVEN a lot . . .

This is not new, I might add. I have thought about heaven a lot for well over half of my life. What most don't expect in life happened to me. At thirty years old, my life, my nuclear family, was completed truncated, suddenly, unexpectedly, one night with no warning. When the phone call came at midnight I was awake, watching, hoping, praying, and I confess generally believing that things would work out, as they always did, somehow. That was not to be the case, and when the pastors came to tell me that they had found my husband's body, I and my two little boys, one six years old and only a week from first grade, and my nine-month-old baby, entered a whole new element of life's experience. Dare I even utter the words so boldly, "death experience"?

While our house seemed to fill up all night with family arriving, having traveled through the night, and friends from church bringing love and comfort, I found myself alone for a time upstairs in the master bedroom closet touching my husband's clothes. Touching the wool suits, the navy sports jacket, the white shirts, the colorful ties, his neatly folded pajamas, pressing them each to my nose and inhaling deeply, hoping to catch a bit of the precious life that was still vivid in my life. If the truth is that there was only the faintest of aroma, there was nevertheless something else. A presence. A stillness. Quiet. My tears, which had not stopped until then, stopped. The spiritual was there somehow. So quiet. There was silence but not absence.

I was still, motionless, unclear what was happening. In the midst of it, all I could offer was acceptance. "I understand," I said quietly. What did that mean then? A word of comfort to my husband? Acceptance of what the Lord had ahead, perhaps, but I had no earthly idea what I was accepting.

Only a few nights later there was the dream. Vivid. I was walking with my boys in a dystopian woods—perhaps after a forest fire when the smoke had disappeared. Nothing remained but the fragmented trunks of trees and the crunch of the burned foliage beneath our feet. All of the horizon was dark, all around it was ash. I was holding my six-year-old son's hand and the baby on my hip. We were walking into an oblivion, unseen, even foreboding, but mostly just barren and dark. I remember my awareness during that dream as if it had just occurred. Walking together there that night in the landscape view, we were completely alone and utterly helpless. Yet, I thought, I must take these children out of this darkness. How? I had no idea. I would like to say that it was then that an angel appeared or spoke to me or lifted us or delivered us—but that would not be the truth. No. What I recognized as there was just this sense: Keep walking. Keep holding onto the children.

In an experience like that, it is hard to not think about what comes after death, when after experiencing death, there certainly is something there beyond death. I know that.

All throughout my adult life, I have thought about it. I have thought about heaven a lot.

How did I come to this? About six years before, my husband and I had committed ourselves to reading straight through the New Testament without stopping in the month of July. This was an entirely intellectual exercise. We were reading in history and philosophy. This was just part of that ongoing endeavor. We had agreed to read independently each day and discuss each evening after dinner. We planned to be completely finished by July 31. Even though we had each been raised in the church, we had no idea whatsoever what a formidable and frankly dangerous exercise this was. We had progressed only through the first two or three Gospels, and we were believers. It just happened—to each of us. No one was more surprised than we were! We didn't tell anyone for months. Honestly, we didn't know what to make of it. During that time, we prayed, read, studied, sought out sources, and grew in our faith.

So let me tie the thread here between this early part of my Christian understanding to my recurrent reflection on heaven. From age twenty-six, when I embraced my faith wholeheartedly, and while living in the midst of that flush of fresh joy and the power of God's grace, I had not just thought of the beginning of faith. Almost concurrently I could see that the culmination of faith was heavenly. We were going towards something in our Christian walk, and it was not the unseen and unknown but the hope, outlined in Scripture and promised by Jesus, that hope that at some point is seen and known. We were journeying towards God, towards eternity, towards heaven, and we were not going to be there alone. In the midst of the beauty that Revelation describes, in the midst of being with God and angels, we would be with many other believers, family and friends, from our earthly life, yes, and "a whole cloud of witnesses" described by name in the Letter to the Hebrews. This realization has never left me. Heaven was to be a community affair.

Have you ever thought about the fact that not only will your believing family members be with you in eternity, but you may know a few other people there as well? I don't mean just people that you will meet there or people from your ancestral family, or Scripture, or world history, or the history of the church. That will happen, yes. But I mean others whom you have known and loved and shared in *this* life. Your life today.

Now, I'm sure that my beginning the topic of friendship is surprising to most. Yet, in fact, it is perfectly congruent when one thinks about earthly believers' family and friends' relationships of depth and spirituality.

My guess is that most of us have barely given this any thought at all. In fact, you may think to yourself, I haven't heard this exactly this way before. You may think this is fanciful, highly imaginative, wishful dreaming, and difficult to pin down as any sort of truth. You may think that it is really reaching to even suggest that our human relationships, family relationships, and Christian friendships are imbued with an eternal capacity. You may think that unless you take a serious look at Scripture, and I don't mean just the last chapters of Revelation, the last book of the Bible. I mean from the very beginning.

If we know anything about the nature of God as presented in the Holy Scripture, we know that God is *relational*. God, the Triune God, Father, Son, and Holy Spirit, exists in community. God is so relational that God created the world and every aspect of it to companion with him. Everything from light and darkness, sky and sea, birds and fish, heavens and earth, animals and—a human man. God pronounced it all good. Yet, there is one catch. Man does not find someone like himself. There is no other soul to whom the man can relate. Now, the great thing about this is that God completely understands this. God gets it. Why? Because God is relational. In response to man's loneliness, God creates woman as a partner, a helpmate, and equal bearer of the mandate to be sovereign and caretaker of the earth.

In the Advent/Christmas season, we celebrate the coming of God in flesh to be with humanity, to save humanity, to be Emmanuel, God *with us*. We have heard the Christmas story so many times that it may have become ho-hum to us; but think about it. God, in Christ, divested of heavenly prerogatives, emptied himself, gave up most all of it, to be *with us*. Relational.

All through the Old Testament, there is the history of God reaching out to humanity, to Israel, to the people with whom God chose to have a personal relationship. Prophets, priests, and kings all play their divine role in relating to the Hebrew people, bringing a message of God's love and destiny for them, if they will only wholeheartedly embrace the covenant relationship of mutual love and be faithful. It is all relational.

In the Gospels, Jesus, beginning in his earthly ministry, chooses twelve specific companions, disciples, to be *with* him. Relational. Even Jesus doesn't try to go it alone without human friends.

Scripture tells us that there were also women attached to this group of disciples who supported the ministry with money and witness and service. Jesus created an entire small loyal community around him. Relational. In the end, he lost only one from this group, Judas the Betrayer.

Continuing on in Scripture, we have the letters of the disciples/apostles to the various church communities. And what are these letters about? They are about living a life in relationship to Jesus, dealing with questions that have come up in community about what it means to live as a Christian in a pagan world, what it means to live loving God and loving one another in the church, the Christian community. Relational.

When we think of relationships in eternity, we cannot skip Hebrews, which says quite clearly that we are surrounded in this life with a cloud of witnesses (identified believers) cheering us on in our lives, our "race" of faith. Relational. Finally, in Revelation, we see God again in tender relationship with humanity, replacing the broken, sin-filled world with a new heaven and a new earth. Scripture says the place of God will be with humanity, and he will wipe away every tear from their eyes, and sorrow will be no more. God with us in a new heaven and a new earth. That is the culmination of relationship.

Relationality is a major key to understanding God—the creation—your life—yes, your friendships on earth and in heaven. One of the last things that Jesus ever said was about friendship. Jesus famously told his disciples the night before he died that he no longer called them servants—he called them friends. Relational.

The truth is that of all the important things that fill our lives, our relationships—with God—with our family—with our friends—are by far the most important. John Gottman, prominent American psychologist, researcher, and clinician, maintains in his book *Seven Principles for Making Marriage Work*, that those in long-term happy marriages generally cite the key to their marriage is that their spouse is their best friend.[1] Current research shows that people who have, among their circle of friends, one closest friend and four other very close friends live longer and with more joy. You and I, we were made to be in meaningful relationship with others.

From the moment we are born, we are reaching out to touch another. I remember quite well a firstborn instinct in action some twenty-plus years ago when our niece was born. We were in driving distance of the city where she was born. So, we jumped into our car and drove the five hours to meet our new niece. We knew that my husband's sister and her husband had debated about whether to have a child or not. They had a great life together!

Eventually, they decided to try to conceive, and now, just arrived, was their very new baby daughter. We hurried into the hospital to greet our sister and walked with our brother-in-law to the neonatal area where we were able to peer through the glass and view the newest member of the family. She was screaming her head off!

A nurse glanced up, saw the dad, and motioned for him to enter. He was noticeably hesitant. "Me?" he whispered, knowing she would lip-read his words.

"Yes," she nodded definitively. With a helpless look at us, he opened the door. The nurse met him with a gown. She was determined. He was going to comfort his screaming daughter. He turned to us with a pleading, what-am-I-going-to-do look. Then, with the nurse brooking no hesitancy and motioning him on, he slowly moved to stand beside his daughter's tiny bassinet. She continued screaming, red faced.

Then, something amazing happened. He instinctively put his hand near her little body, and immediately, she reached out and grabbed hold of his forefinger. Her tiny fingers wrapped around his hesitant finger, and

---

1. Gottman and Silver, *Seven Principles*, 19.

she stopped crying. Immediately, she stopped crying! His face literally lit up. Later that day, as he was holding her and standing near our sister, he was beaming. Gone was the hesitancy. Gone was the reluctance, the uncertainty. "Isn't she just perfect?" he said to us. Yes, I thought, she is perfect. With one instinctive gesture of reaching out in relationship, she bonded with her father for a lifetime.

We are made to be in relationship. We are created relational. Like our creator God, who is relational in being, we bear that unmistakable family resemblance. The fact is that human beings are hardwired, from the umbilical cord and throughout life, to be in meaningful relationship with others. So, knowing this, that we are made to be in meaningful relationship with others, let's do a little exploring about what the wisest of the wise have had to say about the subject of friendship.

Now, the fact is that even before Christ, there are some profoundly wise thinkers who continue to inform our Western civilization today. For example, let's start with Aristotle, who was a Greek and lived from 384 to 322 BC. He wrote a lot about relationships, about friendships, and their importance in his *Nicomachean Ethics*, book 8. I have loved the way he categorizes them with such clarity that it helps ascertain and understand our own actions and the actions of others in relationship. Aristotle maintained that all relationships/friendships can be divided into three categories: useful, pleasant, and good. When you think about it, we all have these three categories in our lives.

The useful are those we know and interact with who perform some service for us, usually for payment or some sort of recompense. Your doctor, your attorney, your teacher, your plumber, your hairdresser, your therapist, the checkout person at the grocery, the salesperson at Walmart or Target. These people are populating your life by providing useful services, and you may become acquainted with them and genuinely like them. Certainly, for the most part, you appreciate the service they provide. However, if they didn't provide that service, it's probable that you wouldn't even be acquainted. My guess is that if you didn't call back that same plumber the next time you needed a plumber, his or her feelings wouldn't be hurt. He/she may regret losing the business, but it's not personal. It's useful. Think about a couple of useful relationships in your life. To identify them as useful doesn't mean that you're using them, in the pejorative sense. Useful relationships are beneficial to both parties. That's how Aristotle defines useful.

Now, some of you know that my husband (I eventually remarried) and I moved from San Diego to Wheaton, in the Chicago area, in the early spring of 2016. I can tell you that one of the great challenges of moving to a new state is finding the right useful people for one's life. We needed everything, from a new furnace technician to a new hairdresser, a new doctor, a new grocery store. Once settled, the useful category sort of fades into the background of one's life, but in the beginning of a new environment, it is a compelling issue! Useful is important.

Aristotle's second category is pleasant. These are the relationships that happen along the way of one's life. It's as if they dropped in and stayed for a while. Outside of family, this includes the vast majority of our social lives. This includes all those whose presence you enjoy; perhaps it includes your neighbors if you spend time with them, your golfing buddies, it may include the parents of your kids' closest friends, even some of your colleagues and professional connections. We don't want to live our lives without these pleasant relationships. Nevertheless, for most people, those who populate the pleasant category in our lives change over time. You may enjoy and look forward to being with them, but when circumstances change, well, you may or may not see them very often. You may move from that city and need to take time to identify those who will present themselves in your new relocated life. Outside of family in general, pleasant is predictably fluid. It changes, but it remains pleasant. That's how Aristotle defines pleasant.

And then Aristotle identifies the good relationships. Now "good" for Aristotle is a word of the highest order. It's not like good versus awesome, as we might say today. Good is highly moral and finest of the fine—to use an old word, virtuous. These are the relationships of depth and, in my experience, usually spiritual. These are the closest of the close to you. Yes, these are those you could call in the middle of the night, if there were an emergency—but even more than that, these are the people who really know you, who understand that you are a real person with hopes and disappointments, who realize that some days you are not your best self, but they still love you, and they always point you toward that best in your life. They always hope for the best for you. They are not ambivalent. They never encourage anything shady or sinful in your life. They believe in your best self. They are "all in" in the relationship. Good relationships, as Aristotle defines them, are precious beyond words, and for most of us, there are just a few in our lives. That's how Aristotle defines the good.

So, useful, pleasant, and good. It's pretty easy at any particular time to figure out who is who in one's life. Sometimes these categories overlap. A pleasant relationship in time can grow to the point of good. Another pleasant relationship moves away and the relationship essentially stops. Useful. Pleasant. Good. Three valuable discernment tools for understanding relationships.

However, it was the Roman Cicero, who lived from 106 to 43 BC, who wrote extensively about friendship in a way that impacts us still today in the Christian community. Though Cicero, like Aristotle, was pre-Christian, his thoughts have intersected with our Christian perspective in a unique way. How this intersection occurred is a story in its own right.

The story unfolds in the twelfth century. It seems that there in the court of the Scottish king was a young, very popular, Scottish courtier, with an extraordinary social intelligence, named Aelred. Aelred had come from a long line of faithful Christian priests in the days when priests were allowed to marry. Aelred, in the course of his fine education, had read Cicero's *On Friendship*, which was one of the few available manuscripts at the time. It so happened that when Aelred was in the court of the king, the king gave him a message to deliver to an influential noble in the north. Obediently, Aelred made the horseback journey from York through the hills and forests of northern England. Here is where the ordinary turned extraordinary.

As Aelred came near his destination, he came upon a beautiful valley with a winding stream sequestered by trees and rolling hills, wooded and abundant. There, nestled in the valley, was a newly established Cistercian monastery by the name of Rievaulx Abbey. Looking upon it, he felt an unusual tug of his heart. Overnight, he prayed about it and was filled with a sense of God's call and personal certainty. Rievaulx was the place that God intended for him to be. Upon bidding farewell to his host, Aelred returned for another look at the Rievaulx Abbey. There, once again, he felt that unusual deep sense of destiny for his life. Without doubt, God was calling him there, and there he stayed. He lived there the rest of his life. He left only to travel on official church business. He never returned to live at court.

The influence of that journey and Aelred's subsequent decision to make his life in Rievaulx remains with us today. In time, Aelred became a monk and then later the abbot. Having met Bernard of Clairvaux as a young monk, he heeded Bernard's encouragement to write down his thoughts. So, when Aelred wrote about friendship, he used as a guideline the writings of Cicero on that topic. Aelred took the wisdom that Cicero presented and added to it the scriptural truth corresponding to it. Cicero defined friendship as "nothing else than accord in all things, human and divine, conjoined with mutual goodwill and affection."[2] Aelred, in agreement, took that definition and enhanced it as two friends and Christ. Aelred understood friendship as entirely Trinitarian. Today we have Aelred's marvelous little book entitled *Spiritual Friendship*. Here he explicitly defined Christian friendship as "mutual harmony in affairs human and divine coupled with benevolence and charity [love]."[3] *Spiritual Friendship* contains guidelines on how to form friendships, what qualities to look for, and even more importantly, I think, a description of Christian friendship. Here is the core of what is remarkable about Aelred's writings. Aelred understood friendship as spiritual dynamic. Aelred understood friendship as beginning in Christ, being preserved in the Spirit of Christ, and returning to Christ. Aelred understood friendship as eternal.

Because Aelred defines Christian friendship as a relationship of three parties—the two friends along with Christ—there are powerful spiritual implications. Thus your Christian friendship with someone you hold as a dear Christian friend has the potential to be a friendship that not only brings joy and comfort and encouragement and companionship to each friend, but also brings spiritual growth in depth for each soul. Aelred would maintain that these Christian spiritual friendships may be remarkably similar to other friendships from the outside looking in. Christian friends socialize together, may help you make a new recipe, build a fence, go on an errand to fix the snowblower, or accompany you to find just the right dress for the next big event coming up in your life. But there is one additional aspect. In the midst of a weekend, an evening, or an hour with a Christian soul friend, the conversation could easily and quite naturally include talk about God, such as: *when this happened, I knew it was the Holy Spirit*; or one's spiritual journey, such as: *I am still praying and waiting on what God has in mind*; or even a question asked in confidence: *Are you still on track with your decision to work towards forgiveness?* And from time to time, or regularly: *Can I pray with you about that?* These sorts of friends are known to pray together most everywhere, even on the phone or by text.

Now if you consider that a believer's journey is ultimately to a heavenly life in relationship with God and other believers, the communion of saints, as it is called in the Apostles' Creed, how wonderful is it to have with

2. Cicero, *De Amicitia*, 131.

3. Aelred of Rievaulx, *Spiritual Friendship*, 53.

you your companions, your friends, from your life on earth, those whom you have encouraged in their faith and they have encouraged you in yours. It certainly makes eternity all the richer.

So, when I talk about friendship—when I write about friendship—when I seek to practice Christian friendship in my own life and encourage others to do the same, I do this with the sure knowledge that heaven is very much a part of the equation. When you think this way, it increases your personal joy and sense of meaning of the relationships. Christian friendship is not just useful or pleasant. It is good of the highest order. It is extremely valuable to your soul. It challenges us to be as God created us to be—our best selves—in the communion of saints.

Now, our new friend, Aelred, in his writing, spent considerable time and prayer as he outlined the steps to making friends of this caliber (remember, one doesn't have a lot of these in one's life) and the issues one might face in the course of relationships. So, in addition to our most contemporaneous question—How do we have time to find, make, develop these sorts of friendships?—one must add the challenging fact that these sorts of friendships take a duration of time to develop to maturity, and in addition to that, there can be multiple pitfalls along the way. Sometimes the whole endeavor can seem daunting, especially if you're new in a community.

The good news here is that none of us is starting from nothing. Yes, you may feel lonely right now, but look around. Even if you've just arrived in a new city, remember, we all have some sort of community around us. No matter where we are, there is in some form the body of Christ, a congregation, a church. When you think about it, it's a heaven-sent opportunity! Also, most of us have lived at least ten years, or two or three or five or nine times ten years. Our lives are filled with all sorts of various people. The truth is, you have lots of people somewhere in your life. Cultivating friendship doesn't necessarily mean it just has to be with new people. It may mean focusing and tending and reviving relationships you already have. Paying attention to the people who are already in your life can result in a marvelous benefit in your life.

So, let me introduce you to the four stages of developing friendship that our abbot Aelred of Rievaulx has outlined for Christian spiritual friendship. Don't worry about "old" English. I have updated the words—but not the concepts. According to Aelred, the first stage is connection. We would probably say, "Hey, I met someone today whom I really liked. I don't know. There was something about him/her that resonated with me.

I felt like we could be friends." That's connection. Now, I am guessing that most of us have had this experience from time to time. Probably you've discovered what I've discovered, that not all of these initial connections develop into something more. Nevertheless, more and more as I review my own life, I realize that all of my closest Christian friends are a result of that initial feeling. "I really like this person. I'd like to reach out to them and see if we could be friends."

Of course, there are other ways to be connected. Sometimes it happens through common professional interests. Almost forty years ago now, a couple of my friends from seminary realized that being pastors was going to be lonely, and what we needed to do was to form a national covenant group for clergy of our denomination. They invited a few of us who were connected to them to join them in reaching out to others. Then we each picked some people that we thought would fit well into such a group. Before long we had forty clergy from all across the country. None of us knew everyone. At this writing, we've been meeting now for thirty-four years, for three to four days in various meeting places around the country. We know one another pretty well now. It's turned out to be one of the most important friendship groups in my entire life, and it was a real gamble, of time, of money, and of commitment. It paid off. Connection can be the start of something big in your life. It's important and not something to ignore.

After connection, Aelred describes a time of companionship. It's the getting-to-know-you phase. You reach out. You do things together—like get coffee—go to the game. You share some things about your life. You listen carefully to what this potential new friend shares. You may know right away that you'd like to get together again. So, another meeting is discussed as possible—nothing too definite. It will develop in a few days or a week or a month. Another phone call, another time together. Sometimes people say right away, "I really want to get to know you." If you have a mutual feeling, say so. Still, there's nothing definite here. Nothing committed beyond an initial meeting. Perhaps it will slowly develop into more and more until there is that feeling of familiarity, free and easy conversation and laughter, and perhaps references to faith or faith experiences and the Lord. The companion stage can take a long time. It can easily take a year, three years, five years, or a lifetime. Honoring the depths of another's soul takes patience, care, and kindness. For the most part, relationships can stay in this stage permanently. This isn't an unsatisfactory stage necessarily. It just isn't the most fulfilled of Christian friendships.

In our mid-twenties my husband and I, newly exuberant in faith after having read the New Testament and having come to terms with our new spiritual condition, decided we wanted to study the Bible. We thought it would be even better to do it with others. We invited four other couples our age and stage to join us in our first-ever small group Bible study. We hardly knew any of them, but we had become acquainted at church. That group of relatively young Christians met every Friday night—and I do mean every. It was rare to miss. We studied the Bible. We taught one another. No one was an expert. Everyone was a learner. This lasted two years. What continued to remain additionally significant for me about this experience was the aftermath. That group was the glue that subsequently got me through the initial stages of my widowhood. While the group meetings no longer occurred, at least formally, many in that group stayed closely connected. Five of them, two now deceased, still remain close friends of mine. Two of them are my very closest friends. It started as an initial commitment to study for a while, being companions in our effort. It became for many of us a commitment for a lifetime of friendship in Christ. Companionship emerged not only as a joy but a comfort.

The third stage Aelred designates as commitment. This occurs after a significant amount of time as companions. Both parties realize that they have solidified a Christian friendship that can navigate at the depths of life. It is a true, honorable, blessed intimacy of two souls who do hold one another tight, and don't let one another down, and live honoring God.

In the fourth stage, communion, there are no longer any questions. There is the highest order of trust and pure affection. Few relationships reach this peak—but when they do, it is a blessing for you on earth—and in heaven, although the truth is, we seldom consider that future unexpected blessing.

A few years ago, a spouse of someone in that early small group died. My husband, John, and I drove to Indianapolis from Chicago for the funeral. It was a somber, dignified, and profound service, honoring my friend's husband and lifting up the great truth of Jesus Christ as resurrected Lord. The pastor couldn't have spoken more appropriately and eloquently. With the crowded sanctuary of Tabernacle Presbyterian Church, one could see the evidence of a life well lived as a doctor, a healer. "One has passed from us," the community was acknowledging, "one who has lived among us as a person of faith and charity" (that old word for love).

The next day, many of that small group met at a familiar café for breakfast. "Let's get together before we all head home," I had encouraged. There were eight or ten of us there. I looked around. At the table were seated most of the closest friends of my life. For me, it was one of those moments where time is compressed. At the head of the table sat the new widow who had lovingly nursed her husband through a difficult last-year's battle with cancer. "She's still full of so much life," I thought to myself, "even in this grieving time." As I sat there, I saw her in my mind's eye as a young mom, redheaded, making peanut butter-and-jelly sandwiches for three kids and talking to me about her hypothesis that perhaps one could save more time washing all the dishes at the end of the day rather than after each meal!

Almost as if I were transported, I remembered how we met when I, in my mid-twenties who had just moved to Indianapolis, stood in my new kitchen with my husband's dear mother who said, "You should meet Marion Root [not her real name]. You would like each other." How could his mother have known with such surety? I wondered. Somehow she felt the possible connection for us. Now, so much time has passed. The night my husband died she was with me in the house the entire night. Even when I tried to sleep, she sat in the family room keeping watch, helping to bear my grief. I learned that night that bearing one another's burdens is a real thing.

While I have lived for years around the country but mainly in California, she, with only one time away, has made Indianapolis her lifetime home. I recalled an evening in Los Angeles, picking up the phone and hearing her voice over the line from Indianapolis. It was an urgent, hushed voice on the other end. "Can we talk?" Some years later, after she surprisingly found herself single again, she began to date a local doctor. Someone we all knew. A few years after that, my phone rang again. Would I come to Indianapolis and be her matron of honor? I came, honored to be there. I brought a wedding gift of a large, antique-like wall clock. It's for this time of new life, I said.

Looking at her life now, could I have imagined that she would raise two boys to be Anglican priests? Looking at her life now, could I have imagined her with her dear daughter living nearby and, among her three married kids, twelve grandchildren? Life turned out to serve a full cup—even with the parched places—the ultimate result, thank God, is full, blessed, God honoring, faithful journey keeping, much loved. When we had each sat in the same front pew of Tabernacle Presbyterian Church in Indianapolis during our husbands' funerals, how could we have ever imagined our lifelong joint journeys?

I must have been lost in thought, as I was swept up in a flood of memories of my friend. Suddenly the clatter of the restaurant snapped me back to the present. I realized that people were getting up from the restaurant table, hugging one another, speaking of the next time together and then saying goodbye. I would say goodbye and love you, too, but I knew that none of us saw it as a real goodbye. Not really. There are no final goodbyes for Christian friends.

Heaven awaits . . .

2

The Good Life

It was October, and my four-year-old grandson was excited about his Halloween costume. This year he was to be a fireman, his dream come true. So, of course, he was enthusiastically dressed head to toe as a fireman—complete with a red jacket and red pants and a plastic ax and a flashlight on his belt. He had chosen to wear his red plastic fireman's hat backwards. His older sister had told him his hat was on backwards. Still, he wore it backwards. Now he was in his car seat, belted in, and we were on our way to the preschool Halloween parade.

When our car approached the preschool, we dutifully entered the designated car lane where we were to slowly pull up to the ramp entrance where the teachers would signal us to approach. While waiting for the prescribed signal, suddenly he asked, "Will the other kids wear their costumes to school?" Surprisingly, he sounded concerned.

"Yes," I reassured him, "The parade will take place as soon as school starts."

"Is this costume okay?" he looked again at his red jacket and red pants with yellow stripes.

"You look just like a fireman," I reassured him again.

He was taking it all in as we waited in the preschool's line of cars. Finally, after what seemed like an eternity of all of five minutes, his teacher signaled us to approach. Then she appeared at the car door. The fireman occupant of our car obediently took her hand, and wearing his hat with summed-up confidence, he walked into school.

We didn't see him again until about fifteen minutes later when my husband and I were standing on the sidewalk waiting for the parade to begin. Then, I looked up, and there our grandson was coming down that long block, first in the line of preschoolers. All sorts of parents and grandparents were standing on the walk complete with their camera phones ready for the perfect moment. As he came towards us, gone was any hesitant concern about his costume. After all, he had been chosen as the leader of the whole parade! Now he walked like the real fireman he hoped to be. As he came towards us, I thought he might call out as he walked past, but keeping his dignity, he refrained. The only thing that gave him away was a little smile as he turned his head just ever so slightly to be sure that I saw him. This was a dream come true for him.

After school on the ride home, my grandson reflected on his experience. "You know I'm not a real fireman yet, Deedee" (my grandmother name).

"I know," I answered.

"I can't climb the ladders," he said.

No, not yet," I agreed.

"But when I'm a man, when I'm a man," he repeated himself for emphasis, "I will be a real fireman." He continued, "I will be a really good fireman."

"Of course," I said, rather absentmindedly.

"No, Deedee, a really, really *good* fireman." He said this with an emphasis on good. "I will save people," he said earnestly. "Like a *good* fireman!"

"I think you will," I responded.

Then he continued. "Firemen have to be strong, Deedee."

"They do," I agreed.

"When I'm a man, will I be strong like Daddy?"

"Just like Daddy," I said.

My grandson smiled at the thought. He would be a really good fireman, strong like his daddy and able to climb ladders. But then he said something that surprised me. "I'm going to be a good fireman, Deedee."

"Yes, I know you'll be good," I said.

"I will be good at ladders and saving people."

"Hmmm," I nodded.

"No, Deedee, *really* good."

"Oh, I know," I said, hoping I was adequately acknowledging his comment.

"Good—not just climbing ladders, but good like Daddy." (Daddy is not a fireman.)

"You mean like a good man?" I asked him.

"Uh-huh," he said suddenly lost in his thoughts. "Good like Daddy," he murmured quietly.

In that millisecond a fleeting thought occurred to me. I couldn't help but wonder, as grandmothers do. Could this have actually been a conversation in the car with an almost-five-year-old when I had simply brought him to a Halloween parade? Could he have intuited the difference between good at doing his job and good as a man, a difference between doing and being? Time will tell, but for now, in his dreams, he was headed for a good life.

There is something we should ask ourselves: What is my dream for a good life?

I remember quite well when I was around five, just about the age of my fireman grandson, when my mother and I were taking a walk. She was telling me about growing up and what joys there were in life ahead for me, (I remember her emphasizing that I would graduate from college), when she stopped, bent down, looked into my eyes, and said, "You are going to have a good life!" Her smile framed her prophecy with joy. I took it all in.

"I am going to have a good life," I said to myself, "there is no doubt about it." That day my mother gave me a great gift, a lens through which to understand my life, framing it as good. I never forgot it.

Still, it's not just a prophecy or a wish or a hope that makes for a good life. Jesus emphasizes that there is always a foundational choice one must make. That choice determines what sort of person one will be and what sort of life one will have. He uses an example of two gates or two ways to enter a city. One gate is broad and ends up leading to destruction. The other gate is narrow and leads to life (Matt 7:13–14). The implication is that the narrow gate leads not only to life, but to "abundant life" (John 10:10), another promise Jesus makes about life.

Certainly, one key aspect of the abundant life is friendship. Aelred of Rievaulx, our English twelfth-century monk, emphasized that friendship is a manifestation of virtue (read: goodness), being a manifestation of spiritual giftedness. In other words, the ability we all have to make friends is a gift from God. The gifts of the Spirit have different emphases in different personalities. In Gal 5:22 Paul lists the gifts of the Spirit as love, joy, peace, patience, kindness, goodness, faithfulness, gentleness, and self-control. In all sorts of different ways, different Christians at different times exhibit one or more of these gifts. Aelred emphasizes Jesus's words that there is no greater love than a man laying down his life for a friend (John 15:13). Here we see, just like in 1 Cor 13, that love is the greatest of all the expressions of the gifts of the Spirit, and love overcomes all. This is important in the relationship of friendship because the fundamental basis of Christian friendship is pure, godly love. That is the singular characteristic that allows friendships to continue throughout a lifetime. Your friend may be a marvelous and virtuous (i.e., good) human being, but no friend is perfect. It is then that love mediates throughout the relationship and gently overcomes the rough places in the friendship.

Contemporary writers emphasize the significance of friendships for an abundant life. Jordan Peterson, in his recent book *12 Rules for Life*, writes in rule 3: "Make friends with people who want the best for you."[1] At first it sounds selfish, doesn't it? We may ask, What about the people who need our help? Peterson points out, quite rightly, that friendship is a "reciprocal" relationship. It's not a rescue party. I would add that there are multiple other types of relationships for those who require saving, but friendship, real friendship, is a relationship that builds up and encourages both parties in their best, their good lives. There is a legitimate love for neighbor in a close friendship. Any lurking jealousy is quickly overcome with genuine love. Peterson ends his chapter by emphasizing the difficulty of making good, virtuous friends for one's life. Notice he doesn't say "perfect people."

He writes this: "Don't think that it is easier to surround yourself with good healthy people than with bad unhealthy people. It's not. A good, healthy person is an ideal."[2]

That is why if you have a handful of good friends, whom you would trust with most everything in your life, or even two or three good friends, you have a wealth of riches for any life in the friendship category.

Still, we ask: What makes for a good life? Cicero and Aelred would tell us that a good life is a life that cherishes a few good friends. When we as secular contemporary people think of the good life, we tend to think of living a life that has accumulated wealth and power. We almost can't help it until we take time to consider that, in fact, neither of these things necessarily brings about the good life.

1. Peterson, *12 Rules for Life*, 82.
2. Peterson, *12 Rules for Life*, 83.

Christians have long understood the good life to be a life that is conformed to the image of Christ (Rom 8:29) by loving God with all one's heart, soul, mind, and strength, and our neighbors as ourselves (Matt 22:34–49). Early philosophers and Christian theologians have described that process of living the good life as an embracing of faith and the virtues of life, in juxtaposition to the vices of life.

You may be wondering what the virtues are exactly. There are seven. Aristotle and Plato embraced what are called the cardinal virtues. These are wisdom (the key virtue and its fruits), temperance, courage, and justice. The early church fathers also embraced these cardinal virtues and added to them the three theological virtues of faith, hope, and love.

The cultivation of the virtues in one's life is the cultivation of formational factors. They are not only enhancers of character and life's happiness on a single occasion; the embracing of a virtue in your life opens an avenue of steady development for the whole of your life. The truth is that practice contributes to mastery. A ten-year-old child who chooses to do what is good to a classmate on one occasion has a head start in developing into an adult who may find themselves in a position to contribute good to a whole family, a whole company, a whole community, a whole country. Virtues don't generally arrive full blown. They develop. They grow. They expand in goodness to others, and they promote a personal good life.

I realize that some of this language itself may feel obscure to us today. In our current Western culture, when we think of the virtues, we tend to think of them as old-fashioned. We may think of them as prohibitions, limiting our freedom. However, that is a misunderstanding. The virtues are not so much about what to do or what not to do. The virtues are about what or who we want to be. Embracing the virtues is the avenue to living the Good life, the abundant life in Jesus's words. Jesus told his followers, "I have come that they may have life, and have it abundantly" (John 10:10b).

The New Testament through the words of Jesus and the New Testament writers offers us many insights into this pursuit of a good life. Christians throughout the ages have understood them as rooted in love, the love of God and the love of neighbor. This love is nurtured in the practice of the regular spiritual disciplines (or practices) of biblical reading, prayer, fasting, meditation, worship in community, participating in the sacraments, and the multitude of ways of demonstrating love for one's neighbor and our world. Faithful Christians practice these disciplines and find significant and formational help and strength for cherishing their life in Christ.

There is also another practice, one could call it a discipline, that was for centuries considered significant that has, at least in the last one thousand years, become minimized. This book is written to highlight that happy spiritual practice—the practice of friendship. Friendship is one of the great keys to learning to practice love, to grow in virtue (goodness), and to experience the good life.

Aristotle, near the end of his life, maintained that individual friendship is central to a virtuous (good) life. Aristotle, of course, was pre-Christian, but significant in the understanding of wisdom nonetheless. We would understand from Aristotle that even in early philosophy, this realization that human friendship was a requirement for the good life was understood and lifted up. However, somewhere along the trajectory of the teachings of the philosophers and the teachings of the church over the centuries, human friendship began to be less emphasized as an important factor for a good life and personal spiritual formation. Today, unless one is searching specifically for this topic, it is challenging to find spiritual friendship among what we might consider the current "spiritual" writings, and it is certainly a challenge to find it emphasized. You may find it, but for the most part you won't find it featured prominently. Friendship as a significant spiritual practice for the good life is almost never highlighted.

So, how do people become what they become? How does a person embrace the virtues? How does a person develop a good life?

Interestingly enough, the truly good and abundant life is significantly discovered and enhanced through human relationships. God made us to be in relationship with one another. When that element is neglected as important, we find ourselves isolated, lonely, self-absorbed, eventually depressed, and even, in the most extreme cases, self-destructive. Certainly God put us in families for a reason. We are not alone. Yes, sin intruded. Nevertheless, human beings innately yearn for the safety and companionship of the family. We saw the damage that was done to many who experienced little human contact during the pandemic of 2020. Virtual contact was better than nothing, but so many suffered from the lack of "skin" in their lives.

There's an old story about a little boy who complained to his mother that he wanted someone to sit with him while he went to sleep.

"Well, you have all your stuffed animals," she said, looking around the lineup of stuffed toys on his bed, "And you know Jesus is always with you."

"No, Mommy," he said, "That's not enough. I want someone with skin on!"

The thing is, isolation cuts deep within us. In fact, isolation quickly becomes a synonym for loss. During the pandemic, we saw pictures of adult children looking through a window at their parent who was in a quarantined nursing home. We had neighbors in the service industries who lost much of their livelihood because stores were closed. We knew of the massive numbers of people seeking unemployment compensation. At times of being threatened by the virulent virus, we were afraid for ourselves, our parents, our children, and our grandchildren. We yearned for the old life, the ordinary life, face to face with parents, with extended family, with friends, with others. We missed the life in our communities. A friend told me on the phone that while it is a gift to be able to worship virtually, "I miss my pew mates." Real life in Christian community is the key to reminding us who we are and encouraging us to continue to live into the abundant life that Jesus has promised. David Benner writes, "The God who is divine community is known only in human community."[3]

You may be thinking: So, is she suggesting that one of the most important spiritual practices in my life is how I maintain my relationships with everyone in my life, how I maintain my Christian spiritual relationships, how I cherish my family, my closest friends in Christ, my soul friends? How I love my neighbor as myself? Yes, that is precisely what I am suggesting.

Sociologists, noticing the importance of human contact in daily life have highlighted a behavior they have labeled "social snacking." This emphasizes the importance of even the most casual contact with others. My husband is an expert in social snacking. If you were with him at the local grocery store, you would notice that he speaks to every checker, every bagger in his checkout line. He knows several of them by name. He's been doing this for years. Would you be surprised that they all greet him when he comes into their grocery line? The actual individual interactions are very brief, e.g., thank you, good to see you, how are you doing. For some of these checkers he is the one to whom they may say: "I only have two more hours in my shift." "My husband lost his job, and I don't know how we're going to make it." "My son is graduating from high school tomorrow. He'll be the first one in our family." "My baby is sick, and I had to leave her with the sitter." And sometimes, knowing my husband is a pastor, "Will you pray for my son? He is struggling with drugs." What began as a purely transactional interaction (i.e., please add up the total bill, please bag my groceries) becomes, as it should be, a human connection. Everyone feels better, *is* better,

3. Benner, *Gift of Being Yourself*, 52.

because they are recognized and appreciated as persons. We all need kind human interaction in our lives. Not every interaction has to be extensive or intimate or instructive or anything other than recognition of the other as a fellow human being.

Out of curiosity I listed the number of human contacts that we had in two, mostly-retired, given days. I was surprised at the total number. So come with me into a description of everyday life that will lead us into a fuller understanding of what it means to begin to focus for good on our relationships with our family, our neighbors, and others. This focus helps us grow in our understanding of one element of the good life. I challenge you to do this for yourself.

To start with, let's think about an average day in our lives and the various relationships we encounter in the course of that day. You may be surprised at what you discover about your own life. The day I describe here is not a day that is dedicated to anything unique. It is ordinary, as most of all of our days are. Bear with me in this detail and you will discover the point I am making.

For example: One day this week I was at home working on a talk I was scheduled to give in a month. My husband, who is partially retired, made scrambled eggs and raisin toast for breakfast. A cleaning lady, an immigrant from Poland, who comes twice a month, came for three hours that morning. Then, the painter whom I have used a few times since moving into our house came for touch-up projects. In the early afternoon our adult daughter and her husband brought over their three children. I have a grandmother's enthusiasm for each of them. So, this was a delight, but it was a writing day for me, so I set them up to play tea party with the plastic tea dishes we had purchased at Disneyland. After an hour, they pronounced themselves bored because I was writing, and they are accustomed to my playing hide-and-seek, tickle, and Sheriff Callie. So, we played. In the meantime, the mail carrier came by, and he and my husband chatted briefly. After my grandchildren left with their parents, I received three meaningful texts. One was from a former parishioner at my church in Pennsylvania asking for prayer for her husband and updating me on his condition. One from a former student at the seminary checking in when would be a good time to talk. One from a friend locally saying she hoped I was doing better after an injury. Later my husband and I went for a quick dinner at a local Italian restaurant. Back at home, my closest friend phoned. My husband skimmed through Netflix offerings. Bedtime came and time for prayer and sleep.

So, let's just consider the various relationships that were in play in my life that day. My husband, the cleaning lady, the painter, my children and grandchildren, the mail carrier, three texts of importance, the restaurant waiter, and a long talk with my best friend—all in addition to my spiritual relationship with the Lord. Fourteen people in the course of one day, and this had been a quiet day for me, a writing day. Family and friends and servicepeople, all of whom in their own very everyday way make my life a more fulfilled life, all of whom in one way or another challenge me to be a better person, kind, appreciative, generous, loving, prayerful, more virtuous, and therefore experiencing my life as good as well as contributing to a good life for each one in my personal relationship orbit. Now before I go any further, some of you may be saying, well, I clean my own house or we do our own painting. I get it, but maybe you wouldn't do that if you were a senior adult. For some of us at certain times in life, some efforts are beyond reach and these kind servicepeople are a gift.

At any rate, the point of my elaborate description of the day's relationships is that these connections are not unusual, not extraordinary. No one at our house received a phone call from the State Department inquiring of our thoughts on the prevailing international situation. *Time* magazine did not come by to take a cover picture of me for their next issue. The pope did not consult with me the other day. Publishers Clearing House did not ring my doorbell. These connections I am describing, or ones like these, are ones that most of us have—family, colleagues, servicepeople. Everyone has lots of connections, lots of relationships with others. All people associate with others in some way—partners/spouses, children, various family members, servicepeople of all sorts. If I had described a day I had as a young mother with preschoolers, or a day I had with other moms in a playgroup, or a day I had as a pastoral counselor at the counseling center or as a pastor, or a day I had as a seminary professor, I would include here the category of colleagues, or clients, or parishioners, or students. Notice that of the fourteen counted, only half of them are relationships that are close to my heart: my children and grandchildren locally are five, my husband, and my closest friend. A total of seven. Notice that of the fourteen relationships, the remaining half also contributed to my life and my experience of a good life. They are not unimportant or to be dismissed. They are contributors to the flow of our days that make life good. Often they become people we care about and with whom we develop a cordial, a friendly relationship.

While we can be friendly with everyone with whom we connect, not everyone is a friend. There is a significant relational confusion that is prevalent in our culture today. Certainly, everyone should be treated in a friendly, respectful manner. Perhaps you've read of the cultural discussion going on today in the United States about the compelling need to reintroduce civility into our daily interactions with others. Civility is nothing more than what used to be known as good manners and polite speech. Civility recognizes that all of us in a family, in a community, in a country, in the world are connected in some way in this global planet that is our home. Ultimately, civility recognizes that every interaction contributes to the peace of the world. Yes, I said, the peace of the world. To be civil is to recognize and honor the common bond, the common dignity, the common heritage that we each have on this earth. The disintegration of civility in a culture is a first step toward the disintegration of a culture. Civility, and the significance of civility, cannot be overstated. Whereas civility is crucial for the building of good will in a society, it is only a first step towards the relationship we call friendship.

To be a friend is to assume a quality of relationship that goes beyond transactional, as with service providers. To be a friend is to be committed from your heart to another's well-being. To be a friend implies a loyalty and affection that ancients historically considered the highest of commitments in human life. Jesus himself, on the night he was arrested, turned to his disciples, and we might imagine, full faced, and with an earnestness that possibly caused them to draw their bodies forward towards him in an attentive position, Jesus himself said: "Tonight I call you my friends," not my disciples, or servants, or acquaintances, or fellow travelers. "Tonight I call you my friends" (John 15:15).

In the ideal sense, the best friendships, especially among adults, take place only between and among people who are committed to living a life sharing together and honoring all that is good (or virtuous) or the best in their lives. Jordan Peterson, the popular author I mentioned earlier, in his book *12 Rules for Life*, emphasizes that true friends are not people who seek connection to one another for any other motive than that they see in one another something that draws them together, some quality, some value, some interest that they mutually share. That initial spark of interest can take place often almost immediately. This is true for young and old. It is a hardwired human "radar." Interestingly enough it is there for all— the best of people and the worst. It operates outside of human volition or often conscious recognition. It just happens. When it happens, we know it. There's an old saying that birds of a feather flock together. My guess is that this human instinct is the basis for that truism. This "hint" is the impetus to a developing friendship.

Significantly, true friendship is the opposite of selfishness. Friendship, in fact, is an embracing of the other to such an extent that selfish desires are supplanted for what is desirable for both friends. There is a deep mutuality in friendship. It is a key element that constitutes a good life.

I will maintain that it is of the highest importance that we embrace a life of friendship. In fact, a life of friendship is the gift of a lifetime. Friendship is not just a luxury. It is a lifeblood.

How is it that in friendship we learn to develop goodness that brings a good life? It is never done in the abstract or in isolation. Consider that the friendship relationship has several important dynamics at work that form us in our character and in our approach to faith and life. The reason that this is so is that human beings were made from their very genesis to be in relationship—relationship with God and relationships with one another. As I have said before, the need and desire for relationship is hardwired into our very makeup. It is part of our operating system. In fact, despite all of my individualistic musings about myself, I cannot know myself unless I am in relationship with others. So, there is a great personal benefit in engaging in friendship, because friendship naturally causes us to probe our limits and grow and mature as we are stretched beyond our selfish perspectives to appreciate and cherish others. This natural deepening that occurs in relationship creates a profound personal satisfaction and a deep inner human knowing.

Of paramount importance is that friendship challenges us. Friendship causes us to grow and mature as we combat the brokenness of our own sinful nature, so that we become more whole. In friendship, we come face to face with the selfish nature that lurks within us. A close friendship can easily bring one or more of the seven deadly sins to the forefront of our mind, tempting us with pride, envy, anger, sloth, greed, gluttony, and lust. These are combated only with the fruits of love expressed in the virtues of humility, kindness, patience, diligence, generosity, abstinence, and purity.

Here's the key: we reach for these virtues within ourselves for the sake of maintaining the friendship. When we do that, we develop into stronger, more loving human beings. We are being formed for the good, and that forming results in the good life.

Friendship affords us joy, companionship, love, insight, and wholeness. There are certain aspects of character in our friend that are attractive to us. We are drawn to them. There are reasons for that. Those things that draw us have reflexive elements in our own lives. To a certain extent, we can see valuable aspects of what we dream of for ourselves in them, and they do in us as well. This encourages us as we encourage one another to be the best we each can be. So we learn how to live, and in the process we are deepened and blessed. We are formed into more mature, healthy, human beings who understand firsthand the beauty of self-giving love in friendship.

As I reread this chapter, I realize that all I have written could seem impossible to achieve. There are too many abilities, too many virtues, too many gifts of the Spirit, or even in some locations too few opportunities for friendships in our everyday lives. We may feel trapped in the same old, meaningless humdrum of life. We may feel trapped with the door shut to us in a multitude of ways. Life is not joy upon joy, and there seems to be no happiness to be found. It can be like that, I know.

Years ago, as a young pastor, I once had a parishioner who would reflect these feelings. To that extent, she had trouble carrying on a conversation—even at church where she was known. She was a kind and giving person, but full of self-doubt and fear. In counseling with her we worked out some initial conversation starters, just a few sentences following a greeting. The really scary part for her was that she had to find a job. After some effort, she found the only job available—a job as a receptionist. Privately, I thought it was perfect. She had to talk to everyone who came in the door. Still, let me confess. I had no idea of the fullness of life that it would present. It's a long story, as life stories go; but in time she ended up leading a citywide agency that brought lifesaving assistance to many in the city. She was known and respected and surrounded with colleagues and friends. She is retired now, but I'm certain she would tell you that in spite of some difficult times in life, she has had a good life.

Another story. Once, years ago, when I was a student in a large graduate school there was a young woman, a Christian, who suffered from cerebral palsy. It was difficult for her to talk, to walk, to feed herself, to do most everything. Yet, ever cheerful, she was in classes that prepared her for an advanced degree. Perhaps out of kindness and perhaps out of admiration, other students in her classes began to befriend her, to include her, to listen to her as she struggled to speak. At graduation at one of the most prestigious locations in the large city, the entire auditorium was in a hush as she struggled to move across the stage to receive her diploma. As she reached out to receive the diploma the entire place stood and erupted into applause. Everyone recognized that what we were witnessing was a hero! It was a sacred moment. It was a moment of recognizing one who had achieved, in spite of staggering limitations, a good life.

Some people face tremendous obstacles in life. Some suffer terribly from illnesses or destructive relationships. The truth is that no obstacle can keep us from a relationship that embodies God's love. We are reminded in Rom 8:38–39 that nothing can separate us from the love of God:

> I am certain that nothing can separate us from God's love: neither death nor life, neither angels nor other heavenly rulers or powers, neither the present nor the future, neither the world above nor the world below—there is nothing in all creation that will ever be able to separate us from the love of God which is ours through Christ Jesus our Lord. (GNT)

I say this to myself many evenings before I go to bed: "Nothing can separate us from the love of God in Christ Jesus our Lord." Friendship, true friendship, is from God. Nothing can separate you from that, the good life.

3

Friendship with God

Living as a Friend of Jesus

LET'S TALK ABOUT LIVING as a friend of God. The Trinitarian God, Father, Son, and Holy Spirit. Some find it helpful to think of the Father as Creator, the Son as Redeemer, and the Holy Spirit as Sustainer. It is hard to consider the Trinitarian God who seems so remote as a friend. For most of us, it seems almost impossible. You may be wondering, is there any other effective way to think about this?

It seems to me that we would find it easier to clarify our topic of friendship with God as living as a friend of Jesus. We can, at least, get some sort of mind's picture of Jesus as a man, as someone humanly relatable. Being a friend with Jesus maybe would be easier if we lived at the same time, if we were one of the twelve disciples or one of those men and women who followed him and supported him. Maybe. The truth is that for most of us living as a friend of Jesus feels like a complete long shot. Is this even possible?

There's an old story about a pastor who was teaching a Sunday School class full of eight-year-old kids. She had explained to them that Jesus loves them and wants to walk closely with them in their lives—and then she resorted to the general way that adults explain this to children. "Jesus wants to be close to you, so close, in fact, that Jesus wants to come into your heart."

The class was silent. It took just a moment for this to sink in. Then, one perplexed eight-year-old asked the obvious question: "But, Pastor, how does he fit in there?"

When we try to engage spiritual realities, we tend to slip into what we can see and touch, the natural physical realities around us. So, when we think of being a friend with Jesus, we think, how can I hang out with Jesus? Go to work with Jesus? Meet my friends with Jesus?

Talk about something that is bothering me with Jesus? It seems impossible or, dare I say it—really out there. It's definitely not anything you would want to casually mention to anyone. They might think you were, well . . . Let's just leave it at that and turn our thoughts to spiritual realities and the basis of all of life. The basis of friendship. Let us turn our thoughts to love.

A few years ago, my three-year-old granddaughter asked her mother, "Is God three or is God one?"

My daughter, her mother, is a historian and theologian. Still, she sighed. This is a question for the ages. "Remember how I explained to you that God is love?" The little one was listening. "So, God is three persons all encompassed in love. Like a family."

Now, my granddaughter had firsthand knowledge of families as well as firsthand knowledge of love. So her mother's explanation was all she needed—for now. "Oh," she replied. She was satisfied.

Now, to be clear this is not an adequate explanation for theology students or mature theologians, but it is a very basic description of the Triune God.

God is love, and love always seeks to express love. God exists in communal relationship, Father, Son (Jesus), and Holy Spirit. So God understands our desire for love, for relationships, for friendships, because God desires the same. God has created us this way. We were, after all, as Scripture attests, made in the image of God. That doesn't mean we look like God or are little gods. No. It means that we bear the family resemblance, the way one of my grandsons has bright brown eyes like his beautiful mother and her mother. "Look at those big brown eyes," the family exclaims with sheer delight. The family resemblance, once again, has come through. When we express love, real love, we are expressing God's family resemblance.

Aelred of Rievaulx lived a life that exemplified love. In his declining years, when he was often bedridden, the monks of Rievaulx Abbey would come and sit in his room, lean on his bed, talk to him about their thoughts, their struggles, their hopes and dreams of serving God.

At the time of his death, on his deathbed, it was no different. There were multitudes of his monks surrounding him. For them to be near him at the time of his death was a heart's requirement, a requirement of love. Now, if you know anything about how abbots (Aelred was an abbot) governed their monks, it wasn't generally gentle. It was thought that to be a leader of a monastic community required a firm hand. Otherwise, it was thought, the community could get out of hand. Aelred, however, was quite different. He didn't subscribe to that leadership philosophy. Rather, he believed that loving and caring brought about the best in each individual monk.

Throughout his life, Aelred maintained a cherished view of human relationships. He took to heart 1 John 4:16: "We know and rely on the love God has for us. God is love and whoever lives in love lives in God, and God in him." In all of his teaching and writing Aelred was essentially and primarily focused on love, the love of God and the love of our neighbor.

Undoubtedly, Aelred was one of the most significant Christian leaders in Christian history. He was an unusually visionary and insightful leader, an extraordinary personality, an attentive abbot, and profoundly faithful spiritual leader. Aelred was so loved because he cared to love each monk in his charge. By pursuing the meaning of love in his theological studies and writings, Aelred came to affirm that friendship by writing in his book, *Spiritual Friendship*, "Christian friendship begins in Christ, is preserved in the Spirit of Christ and in completion returns to Christ."[1]

Most notably, Aelred famously embraced the dictum that "God is friendship . . . if one embraces the Scripture that affirms 'he [or she] that abides in friendship abides in God.'"[2]

This whole account of Aelred and his example in life as a virtual father to his children (fellow monks) makes me think that perhaps when we think about being friends with Jesus it is best to come to that understanding like little children that Jesus said we must be to enter the kingdom of heaven: "Truly, I say to you, unless you turn and become like children, you will never enter the kingdom of heaven" (Matt 18:3). All of this seems impossible to us unless we keep it simple. Is there an actual way, a realistic way, that we can spend our days with Jesus at work or meet friends, or even talk about something that is bothersome with Jesus? Is that realistically possible? No, but it is spiritually possible. Can we live our daily lives as friends with Jesus? The answer is yes.

There's a little pamphlet written by the late Dr. Robert Munger, who was a much-loved pastor and professor. He pastored the First Presbyterian

1. Aelred of Rievaulx, *Spiritual Friendship*, 53.
2. Aelred of Rievaulx, *Spiritual Friendship*, 66.

Church of Berkeley, California, for years and then became a professor at Fuller Theological Seminary in Pasadena, California, where I was a graduate student. Eventually he became one of my mentors. It was known around campus that if you entered his office, there would be predominately placed a prayer bench. Dr. Munger's trousers were often baggy at the knees. It was obvious to everyone that he was a person of prayer.

Years before, he had sought to answer this question of being friends with Jesus or, to put it another way, living a life with Jesus. He entitled it *My Heart—Christ's Home*. It was just a little pamphlet describing life in Christ, with Christ, in the simplest terms possible. He doesn't describe it as Christ entering your heart—well, not exactly. He pictures it as Jesus knocking on the door of your heart (Rev 3:20) and you letting him in. Would this be something of interest in the theological world, in the everyday world, to adults? As it turns out, it was and it is. Let me sum it up for you in a quick paraphrase.

Jesus knocks on the door of your heart, and you, quite literally, invite him in. He is offered a chair in the living room, and you, delighted to have him there, sit with him and talk. He wants to talk about your life. After a while, you have plans to go out to meet friends, but you can't exactly take him with you, so you apologize and explain that you have an appointment with friends, and you must go. He offers to go with you, but you decline. You think, he would never fit in with these friends. Best he remain at home in the living room. So, you go out, and after a little while, Jesus looks around the living room. He doesn't feel free to explore the house. After all, he hasn't been given permission, so he spends the evening in the living room. It's a nicely appointed room with a Turkish rug, comfortable couch, pleasant lamplight, and a bookshelf filled with books. Jesus looks at the array of titles. Some he wonders about, but he does not mention that to you, his host. When you return home, he is there to greet you and asks how the evening was. "Fine," you say to him uncomfortably and hope you don't have to describe the conversation that took place with those friends. You are tired, you say to him, and sorry, but you have to go to bed. Jesus, always gracious, wishes you a good night's sleep, and you head to your bedroom, relieved that nothing more need be said about the evening out. And so the story goes.

For many weeks, your life continues like this. Jesus is always sitting in the living room, and you pass him whenever you're going out. He offers to go with you, and you politely decline, but sometimes you pause and say, "I'm early. I can sit and chat a bit." You find that you enjoy these chats and come away from them feeling refreshed. This happens more and more. Gradually as your affection for Jesus grows and your trust in him grows, you invite Jesus into each room of your house one at a time. As you do, you realize that there are things there that you wish Jesus wasn't seeing. Of your own accord, you begin to rid the various rooms of your heart and home of certain words you say, certain books, certain television networks, certain computer sites, certain magazines, certain music, certain pictures, and certain friends, and refurnish those rooms with those doing honor to him. It turns out that it is much more enjoyable and fulfilling to have Jesus with you wherever you go and with whomever you spend time. Little by little, you see, you have made friends with Jesus.

That's a loose paraphrase of Munger in a nutshell. I haven't read it in years, but it stays with me. That title, *My Heart—Christ's Home*, penetrates one's life. To the child's question—how does Jesus fit in there?—the answer is: bit by bit, time after time, as your trust and love for Jesus grows. It can happen whenever you open the door and invite him in. For some people, there is the experience of a huge rush to move through the whole house and completely clean it out, but for most people, it is a bit by bit growing of a relationship that slowly begins to enhance your life, bringing joy.

Now, let me add a significant caveat here that is important in learning about spiritual realities. Primarily, remember that Christian spirituality is the result of the Holy Spirit at work in our lives, our souls, our minds. There is a difference among imagination, creative ideas, fanciful ideas, human yearnings, and Christian spirituality. The expression of Christian spirituality is the Holy Spirit leading your soul. So, to be clear, just because you imagine something doesn't make it a spiritual reality. It may be evidence of an overactive imagination!

When the Holy Spirit guides you, there are always hallmarks or proofs that one can employ that help you to sort out God's guidance. Scripture warns us to test the spirits. "Test the spirits to see if they are from God" (1 John 4:1); every spirit that acknowledges that Jesus Christ has come in the flesh is from God. There are three key tests that Christians throughout the ages have employed to test the spirits and gain confidence in the veracity of how they understand the Holy Spirit (the Spirit of Jesus) communicating with them and leading them.

1. Scripture: The first is the most important of all. The Holy Spirit never, ever leads us to do something that is forbidden in Scripture. Discernment here requires a familiarity with and understanding of Scripture

or close association with those who are mature Christians and well familiar with the word.

2. Affirmation: The second is the affirmation of other committed Christians. When confronted with a decision of import, sharing with other spiritual and prayerful Christians should yield their affirmation.

3. Love: The third is love. Examination of your innermost motivation should evidence a deep desire to build up and not tear down the other. Certainly, if the Lord is leading, love will be evident and foundational.

Living as a friend of Jesus has more than anything else to do with loving him and neighbor.

Here's an example about a man who lived centuries ago and how he lived as a friend of Jesus. His example has inspired Christians for several centuries. His name was Nicolas Herman. He was born in France in 1614 and became a lay brother in a Carmelite monastery in Paris. You may be thinking that he had to have had an extraordinary role in the monastery for him to be remembered so many centuries later. In fact, Brother Lawrence, as he was known in the monastery, was the dishwasher. He spent most of his days at the kitchen sink where he washed dishes—for many years. Initially, he had an aversion to kitchen work, but he determined to make this a holy service for many years. Throughout that time, rather than regarding it as monotonous, he made it a personal discipline to see it as a means of godly service to his brothers in Christ. From time to time one of his duties was to travel to a nearby village to acquire wine casks. This was difficult for him because he was lame. Sometimes he had to physically roll over the provisions to get from the back of his boat to the front. All this he took as part of his service for Christ's sake.

In daily life, very literally, Brother Lawrence sought to be a friend of Jesus. In his free time, he wrote down his reflections on all sorts of theological issues that pertained to the Christian life. He desired to keep his mind and will primarily focused on the Lord. In his Sixth Letter he wrote, "I cannot imagine how religious persons can be satisfied without the practice of the presence of God."[3] When Brother Lawrence died on February 12, 1691, his fellow lay brothers and monks combined his writings into a little book entitled *The Practice of the Presence of God*. It is a gem of a devotional, as meaningful today as it was those centuries before.

---

3. Lawrence and Laubach, *Practicing His Presence*, 69.

Let me step back into the times of the Old Testament and the references to those whose faithfulness identified them as "a friend of God." All throughout the Scriptures, the Old Testament and the New Testament, we see the love theme displayed as God reaching out in relational love and blessing. Early on, we see it in Noah and the flood. Noah was one who loved God and lived a righteous life in the midst of a wild and perverted culture that had completely turned its back on relationship with God and spurned God's love. The choices of that population resulted in God's response—judgment with the flood. Yet first, God reaches out to Noah, knowing Noah to be one who loved God. Actually, Noah is really given a chance, a choice for life. God tells him to build a lifeboat, an ark. Noah has to consider whether to do it or not. We could assume that if he had not done it, he would have drowned in the deluge. Whether Noah really understood that or not is unclear, but being one who loved God, and believed God, he follows God's very specific instructions of building an ark in a desert. Now when we think of God's love, note that God did not just save Noah through this. God had him gather a regular menagerie of male and female animals. This isn't surprising when we think of God as one who loves relationally. God didn't leave Noah without those like him either. Noah's wife and children and their spouses were all saved. The God who is love is love indeed.

God's love abounds throughout holy history through Abraham, whom God chose to claim the promised land. Abraham unexpectedly has a deep spiritual experience of God. God tells him that he is to leave his home and go into the promised land. God offers Abraham a covenant of blessing. He will be blessed to be a blessing to all the peoples of the earth, and he himself will have descendants as numerous as the stars in the heavens. Certainly, Abraham's encounter with God is one of those life-changing moments for Abraham. Still, since Abraham has personal volition, one has to assume that in reality Abraham had a choice to obey God. He would have to uproot his family and his entire life, and head out into the desert in search of the "promised land," while trusting that all this will lead to his having numerous descendants. Abraham does elect to do as God has called him to do. The impact of that encounter with God determined Abraham's life's spiritual, earthly, and ultimately heavenly journey.

So, Abraham prepares to leave his home in Ur, which was a thriving population area, to journey across the region to what is still an unknown place. But if even for a minute we're thinking Abraham is traveling on his own, we would miss the significance of his relationships. In fact, Abraham loved his father, Terah; his wife, Sarai; and his extended family. So, not sur-prisingly, Abraham brings Terah and Sarai, as well as his nephew, Lot, and Lot's wife and children, and all sorts of servants and livestock and posses-sions. As it turns out, God blesses Abraham richly in land and material pos-sessions after a rather perilous journey for Abraham and Sarai, now named Sarah. Even when Abraham becomes impatient and tries to take charge of creating his own heir, God still brings about the fulfillment of Abraham's dream through Sarah, the one Abraham loves. Sarah, it turns out, was a key to the whole promise of descendants.

It is instructive for us as we reflect on God's love that Abraham's love for God, which he demonstrates in obedience and trust, causes God to re-spond to Abraham very tenderly. In fact, Abraham is called a friend of God in the Scriptures. We see it in 2 Chron 20:7, when Jehoshaphat stands in the assembly of Judah and Jerusalem in the house of the Lord, saying: "Did not you, O our God, drive out the inhabitants of this land before your people Is-rael and give it forever to the descendants of your friend Abraham?" Isaiah 42:8 and 10 also record this: "But you, Israel, my servant Jacob, whom I had chosen, the offspring of Abraham, my friend . . . do not fear for I am with you." And it is in the New Testament that James writes, "And the Scripture was fulfilled that says, Abraham believed God, and it was counted to him as righteousness, and he was called a friend of God" (Jas 2:23).

It is clear that the key to being a friend of God is believing God.

Of course, God's love does not stop with Abraham. It extends to Mo-ses, a baby Hebrew boy found floating in a basket because his desperate mother was trying to save his life. As it turned out, the palace princess found the baby in the basket and brought him up in privilege.

Eventually Moses understands his roots but not how to live them out in integrity when he sees his people as slaves in Egypt. So, he takes matters into his own hands, is exiled and lonely for decades in the desert until . . . God reaches out to him in the form of a burning bush. Eventually, God tells Mo-ses to go to Pharaoh to obtain the freedom of the Hebrew people. He was not alone though. Moses's brother, Aaron, went with him. It was dramatic with all sorts of signs and wonders, the parting of the Red Sea, the Ten Com-mandments, and God leading the people to the brink of the promised land. It took a while, forty years, for the people to enter the land, and Moses was too old to lead them. Joshua did. Moses was permitted to watch it all hap-pening, and then he died in the company of his old friend, God.

When David appears on the scene, it is 250 years after Moses. David is a shepherd boy and the youngest brother of eight brothers. He is seemingly fearless, slaying the giant Goliath, which earns him a place in King Saul's retinue. He becomes the closest of friends with King Saul's son, Prince Jonathan, and continues in his integrity in spite of King Saul's jealous persecution of him. Acts 13:22 recounts this: "After removing Saul, God made David their king. He testified concerning him: 'I have found David, son of Jesse, a man after my own heart; he will do everything I want him to do.'" David was a man after God's own heart.

Consider this. All of these leaders whom God chose, all of them, were in a friendship relationship with God. They all believed God, and because of their belief, they were able to experience friendship with God. This belief is a condition of the heart and soul. Note that all were, in some way, a precursor to our Lord Jesus. They were a type of what was to come. All of these leaders were saviors of God's people in some sense. Yet, it was never just a me-and-God arrangement. There were always others in the mix who supported, who helped, who cared, who prayed, who risked. The God who is love is a God who provides for human love as well. Only through the power of God's love could these things be accomplished, and only with human companionship and love could the one called carry it out. Noah had his family. Abraham had Sarah. Moses had his brother, Aaron, and his sister, Miriam. David had his dearest friend, Jonathan. No one went alone. God always offers us relationship—relationship with God and with a few other believers.

That is how God works. In relationship.

The greatest example of God offering relationship is, of course, in the coming in flesh of God's son, Jesus of Nazareth. He came humbly, poor, and born to an engaged but unwed mother, Mary. His stepfather, Joseph, had even considered not marrying Mary, until an angel intervened to corroborate her story as a virgin who had conceived a child. The night of Jesus's birth in some sort of a cave or a stable, angels appeared singing in the sky, "Emmanuel, God with us"; shepherds heard their message and found the baby to worship; kings, magi from far-off Persia, saw a star and traveled to worship the baby, bringing expensive gifts, which, presumably financed a subsequent flight to Egypt to avoid the death threats of Herod. To say that the birth of the Christ child was an event would be an understatement. Along and over and above the creation itself, Jesus's birth was of cosmic importance. All of human history and holy history hinged on this event. It changed everything.

How did it change everything? Remember the God who loves? It changed everything because Jesus, embodied, came to be "with us" and demonstrate that astounding love. He was literally designated the night of his birth as Emmanuel, which means "God with us." He came to demonstrate in the flesh the love of God, that love that never stops reaching out to those whom God has created and loved. Suddenly, here he was, the one who was hoped for, looked for, even expected in some far-off sense. He came to show us what God was like and how much God loved humanity.

He lived a life that was staggeringly full of love and mercy and sacrifice. He looked at the found-out adulterous woman, who was about to be stoned, and said to the crowd: Let the one who is without sin start this off. On the last night of his life, as Jesus knew he was facing imminent betrayal and an excruciating death, he had a meal, a Passover meal, prepared for him to eat with his disciples. He told them, "I have greatly desired to eat this meal with you." In the midst of that most precious and tender time when he washed the disciples' feet and looked into the eyes of Judas knowing what he was about to do, in that time, Jesus, his heart brimming with love and emotion, said to his faithful disciples, "I'm no longer calling you servants. I'm calling you friends" (see John 15:15).

Jesus called them "friends." They were those who had been with him and followed him and loved him, as friends do. Now, we know that this friendship extended to them is extended to us, if we can embrace it. There is no doubt that sort of invitation to friendship with Jesus is transformative, and that sort of transformation continues on throughout history. It continues today. The love of God, the friendship of God, continues to reach out, to call out persons and peoples, to manifest the presence and the message of the transforming power of God's love. The love of God is not idle or absent or silent or vanished. The love of God, the friendship of God, continues to reach out, to call out persons and peoples, to manifest the presence and the message of the transforming power of God's love. The God who is "with us" is still with us. Speaking to us of the singular importance of love.

When you understand this "with-us" God, it changes everything in your own life. It changes how you understand your life, not as a random series of events, but as a direction that is ever moving towards the expression of the love of God. And here's an important aspect of this love for our lives. This love is always about relationship, and we cannot learn and develop into those who express that love in our entire being unless we are in loving relationships. Family is usually the first place one learns about love, and for many it remains a constant. Yet, it isn't just family that fills this spiritual development of self. We all need friends who are on the same spiritual journey as we are, moving towards God more fully, being more completely the people God's love intends for us to be. These friends join with us in a profound spiritual journey of development that continues throughout life. Their presence in our lives is part of the gift of love that God gives us as Christians. They are not random people in our spiritual landscape. They are key people. They are not just people we try to fit into our schedules. They are a fountain of the wealth of riches that God is offering to pour into our hearts. If you do not know who your spiritual friends are, start actively looking for them. Your congregation may be the best place for you to look. They are there. It may be up to you to invite them into friendship in Christ.

You and I may not be Moses or David. We may not be Miriam or Sarah. We may not be like Mary, Jesus's mother, or the preponderance of godly women who helped build up the first-century church. We may not be Lydia, the first convert in Europe with a church in her house; or Priscilla, a Roman Jewess, who with her husband, Aquila, pastored the church in Corinth. We think of Phoebe, a deacon and a friend of Paul's. We think of Mary and Martha, two sisters, and their brother, Lazarus, who were close friends of Jesus. Yet, we note they lived and loved and matured and celebrated in the midst of relationship with others. We are missing this today in so many aspects of our lives. We are neglecting this key that opens the door to a deeper spiritual life—friendship with Jesus and friendship with other believers.

The apostle John writes in his second letter to one of his disciples, the "elect lady," something that John himself says is not a new teaching: Let us love one another (2 John 5). John understood that it is in love, as God intended it to be, that life exists and thrives. We have all heard this before, the exhortation to love others. There is much in Scripture about cultivating a loving heart, a loving attitude, a loving nature, a loving action towards God and others. Jesus, when a lawyer asked him what he must do to inherit eternal life said: "You shall love the Lord your God with all your heart, with all your soul, with all your strength and with all your mind; and your neighbor as yourself" (Luke 10: 27).

That all seems straightforward, doesn't it, until a scribe wanting to justify himself asks Jesus: Who is my neighbor? (Luke 10:29), and then it is as if a canon was fired into the universe of humanity's understanding of neighbor. Neighbor is not just those who live next door. Neighbor is not just those who look like us. Neighbor is not just those who do us good. Neighbor is not just those who are socially acceptable. No, not just those.

Jesus tells a rather astonishing story of a man who was on a dangerous road on a journey to Jericho, when he was robbed, beaten, stripped, and left bleeding, presumably abandoned for dead (Luke 10:30–37). Some religious leaders saw him, but didn't stop to help. Maybe they were on their way to meet with the faithful who were waiting for them at the temple. They really couldn't stop, they must have thought. After all, they couldn't even touch the man. He was bleeding. That would make them unclean. Maybe some despised him and walked by without a thought. Maybe some felt sympathy for him, but never mind. They went on about their journeys. As it turned out, there was a Samaritan passing by on the same road who came across the man and literally saved his life. Now, you may remember that the Samaritans were half-breeds to the Jews. The Jews would never have even touched a Samaritan—ever. Just touching a Samaritan would have made them unclean. So, who is the man's neighbor? Jesus asks. Of course, the uncomfortable answer is, it is the Samaritan.

Did the Samaritan return to meet the man he had saved? We don't know. Did they become friends? We don't know. We don't know if the Samaritan was a friend of God. What we do know is that this uncommon demonstration of love is evidence of God at work in the Samaritan's life. Certainly, this love is the first step toward friendship.

While it is true that becoming a friend with God may begin with good works, there are many generous people in the world who don't believe in God. So, good works are indeed good but not by themselves a sufficient way to know God. Relationship, friendship with God has many aspects similar to developing a human relationship. There is seeking to meet God and other Christians by participating in community/church services, getting to know God by reading and studying Scripture. There is praying, which I prefer to call talking with God. When we want to be a friend of God all of these aspects are present in our lives. Primarily Scripture says to believe God, one must believe that God exists (Heb 11:6), and another passage affirms that if you seek God, he will find you (Jer 20:13).

I find that there are seasons of the spiritual life. There are times when God works in ways that reinforce your belief and friendship with God. One such incident happened in my experience of growing friendship with God about ten years ago. I was devoting myself to prayer—not exclusively—I had a ministry, a husband, family, a church—but in those moments I could grab alone, I devoted myself to prayer, particularly expressing my love of God.

It was one night when all was quiet and the house was dark. I stood praying in the living room, a place where I often pray at night, when unexpectedly I began to feel that something was happening spiritually. I opened my eyes to see the air in the room vibrating visibly. It grew in a powerful feeling, a vision. At first I thought I must be imagining it. I must be tired. I must be experiencing a fading of my vision. Still, even as I thought that, I knew I was mistaken. There was so much power in the room. All I could say is: "It is you, Lord." To be clear, this wasn't a peaceful experience either. It was awesome, but it was also frightening. When I began to feel frightened, the vibrating in the air stopped.

I confess that even with this sort of powerful experience, I second-guessed myself. I doubted. The next day I thought, "I will pray in the living room tonight. The night before was just an odd experience. It won't happen again." Still, I continued to test my experience the next two nights, when I was alone. I approached the living room, and the power, the vibrating, returned each time. The following third night, even before I stepped into the room, the power was so immense, filling the room with this vibrating of love, that one had the sense that the room was crowded and couldn't hold anything else. I stood at the doorway of the room, hugging the wall by the doorframe for a while. Peeking around, "I am too afraid, Lord," I said. "I love you, but I am too afraid." Sadly, I didn't step forward, and the room returned to normal. It has never happened again.

I have never heard of this "vibrating air" phenomenon before. Nevertheless, for me it was a profound reassurance of the love and friendship of God. Over time, I have understood this as a bit of an experience of heaven and of eternity with God. Heaven is so much more than any of us can imagine.

It may surprise you to know that the Greeks used four words that we translate into one for "love": *agape*—the love that God extends to us and the love that through God we extend to others; *eros*—the love of physical passion and the love of beauty and the arts; *philia*—the love that we have for our friends; *storge*—the love that is affection for things and people we like.

What Jesus offers us is agape love. It is pure and powerful. However, when we discover the meaning of love as Jesus uses it in the good Samaritan, it is not sentimental. It is a tough love, a stiff definition of love. It is love of God and love of neighbor. It is uncomfortable for most. Too much. Love, real love, is tough as steel. Interestingly, the very heart and core of friendship is love.

When my husband and I moved to the Chicago suburbs from San Diego, we had all sorts of willing friends lend a helping hand—and a helping back. We were packing an entire house and each of our offices. It was a lot to pack and to load into the PODS that we had rented in order to move. Day after day for two weeks, we packed and loaded, day after day it seemed as if it would never be finished. On the second to the last day before we had to vacate our house, we sat on the back steps with half a dozen friends, all of us hungrily eating the sandwiches that another friend had delivered. I sat there, bone tired, feeling, without verbalizing it out loud, that I had never been so tired in my life. When we finished the packing, my husband and I were going to drive our two cars across country. I was dreading the two-day drive.

Nevertheless, as I was sitting on the back porch steps, feeling the warm sun and the ocean breeze, as well as feeling a deep gratitude for those friends helping us, quite unexpectedly, a good friend, one of my faculty colleagues, announced, "Pam, my wife and I have been talking, and we have decided that I am going to drive your car halfway to Illinois. You can ride with John in his car and just rest."

"Oh, I can't ask you to do that," I said wearily.

"You didn't ask," my friend said. "We have been watching you, and you are exhausted. I am driving halfway—then, after a day, you should feel well enough to drive yourself, and I will fly home."

Without even thinking, I felt a tremendous flood of relief come over me along with genuine astonishment. Who does this sort of thing? I wondered—although I knew the answer to that. The one who loves his neighbor as himself.

It is God's love, the love of God in Christ flowing through the world—flowing through us—that is transformative. It isn't a flimsy love. It is a with-us love. Stouthearted. Drive-halfway-across-the-country love. It is a bold and determined and does-not-let-you-down kind of love. That is love. The heart of friendship.

4

The Paradox of Time

TIME IS PARADOXICAL. IT expands and contracts. We exist in it. It determines our days and our nights. It gives us light and darkness. When we are young, it spreads out endlessly like an ocean or the rolling California hills. Days seem to expand. An afternoon of play is an enormity. We look forward to growing up, but we know it will take a "long" time. Time seems endless and the possibilities of the future innumerable. Time is our friend.

But time is paradoxical. As active adults we experience a scarcity of time. We are trying to make the most of our time. Hurrying to be there on time. Needing more time to complete a task. Asking ourselves if we have time. Wanting to have more time to do this or that, to meet this person or that one, to pray more, read more, laugh more. Still, we take time or we try to take time for those who are important in our lives.

I remember as a little child, preschool, visiting my great-aunties in Kentucky where the land and the horses were seemingly of endless supply. With the day's work done, there was the evening of sitting on the front porch, the cicadas singing, my aunties in their rocking chairs and me sitting on the step while they recited poetry to one another and took time to teach me, at four years old, some of Longfellow.

"An educated person knows Longfellow," my Auntie Lillian pronounced. Did I gain my love of poetry from that? When I was four? It seemed impossible until I was reading Shakespeare in college and imagined my Uncle Henry quoting one of the great soliloquies. I was little, young, very young, and for me the times on that southern porch seemed endless. But for them, they were taking time, time to share the enriching joys of life with me. That time was precious to them. Yet, it seemed in those moments that time, with her tender, embracing grasp, rested her head with us, dozed and gently drifted. There was, in my memory now, all the time in the world. For them, weary from a day's work of laundry and cooking and tending to the farm, and probably thinking of getting me to bed, time was limited.

As we all know, time seems to constrict as we exist in it.

But then oddly, almost unexpectedly, time reverses itself. It elongates. It eternalizes. We look forward to what exists beyond earthly time. For Christians this means the hope of eternity, of fulfilment in God, the new heaven and the new earth, a release from pain and suffering (often the experience of those near the close of this life), a reuniting with loved ones who have gone before—with only one wrenching caveat for most of us—the pain of saying goodbye, for a while, to those close to our hearts.

As adults advance in age, often those in their eighties or nineties or the chronically ill, time cradles us. It tells us the clock is ticking on our time on earth. Faith tells us we are ready for the next great adventure, eternal life.

In the end, time is our friend again.

These reflections bring me to the great questions about making friends and keeping them: What is it that makes it so difficult for us in any age or stage? What is the single biggest universal impediment to making and keeping friends?

It's time.

❧

From the surveys I have done among contemporary adults to the writings of the ancients, it's all the same tune. Not enough time.

At first I was surprised to discover that this was the plight of people before living life became inextricably intertwined with the flood of communication avenues we have now. Imagining living hundreds of years ago, it seems that there would be time—or at least more time.

However, Aristotle, for example, six hundred years before our Lord, wrote about the importance of taking time to be assured of a real friendship. He warned, "Wishing for friendship comes about as something quick, but friendship does not."[1]

1. Aristotle, *Nicomachean Ethics*, bk. 8, 148.

Every Christian writer reflecting on the development of friendships points to the same truth. Friendships, real friendships, not just social friendships, but serious, heartfelt, soul-deep Christian friendships, take time. Lots of time. That is why most people, at any age, can only manage a handful of them. In addition, the truth is that for most people, the older they get, the more friends they have accumulated, the less time they have to make fresh, new friendships of depth. Because, again, friendships take time.

Now, most people have a whole host of social friends throughout life. These friends are almost always a very pleasant experience. There's not too much commitment or intimacy or obligation. Social friends favor getting together, having fun, talking about the light side of life, laughing, having a meal together. These friends are wonderful to have and usually a relaxing diversion. As I mentioned earlier, these are "come and go" friends, in and out of our lives in certain periods of time. They come—for example, when they move into the neighborhood. They go—for example, when they move out of the neighborhood. Life rolls along. It was fun while it lasted. No one is brokenhearted. They're social friends. We bless them on their way and hold them fondly in our memory and perhaps exchange Christmas cards. They meant a lot to us at one time. They are not forgotten, but their active place in our lives and ours in theirs is usually at a close.

There are, however, friends who last forever, and by that I mean, through this life and the next—into eternity. They are soul friends. Again, these are just a few in any life. If we have three or four or five of these, we are wealthy beyond measure in the friendship department. If we have three or four or five of these, one thing is clear. We have taken time—lots of time— to engage with each of them, spend time with them, listen to them, share our hearts with them, care for them, let them care for us, pray with and for them, bond with them. This may take place over the course of years—five, six, seven, eight, twelve years is not too long to determine if you really have a friend. Or, this may initiate itself in a fairly intense time, of daily or almost daily interaction, lots of face-to-face time and sharing, discovering how much you have in common.

In our highly mobile transient society, some of us have deep soul friends whom we see only every few years and talk to only once or twice a year. Nevertheless, the bond that was formed when we were together seems to be elastic in time. You know those friends who are going to be unexpectedly in town. "Can we have dinner before I catch the plane?" they text you. The answer is always yes. So they drop by, and you start right up where you dropped off the last time. These friends, even if they can visit for just an hour, will find time to reflect something about their faith to you, as they recount their own story. For example—"I prayed for the Lord to make a way for me, and it happened!" Without exception they never fail in the briefest of visits to look you straight in the eye and ask: "So, how are you? How are you really?" Standing on the front porch, with the airport taxi in the driveway, you can say in two minutes with complete confidence that they will understand, "I'm okay. Feeling better. Made the move okay." Or, "So afraid about my job or my kid or my husband's diagnosis. Pray for me." When that happens, you know. That's the interaction of soul friends.

Whether soul friends are near or far, the basics of a Christian friendship remain the same. Real affection or love for one another, mutual respect, wanting the best for one another, encouraging one another, praying for one another, refusing interloping destructive behaviors like gossip, jealousy, competition, betrayal, any sort of association doing harm to one another or those we love. Whereas there are types of friendship bonds between and among those who embrace unethical behavior, they are never truly deep. They will never hold. Their foundation is sand, which shifts willy-nilly. As the old saying goes, there is no honor (friendship) among thieves. On the other hand, friendship among those who are seeking for the good in their lives and in the lives of their friend, those who are wanting their lives to be a reflection of the love of Christ, those whose love for one another in Christ is unshakable, and who have the personal faith and character to hold to the biblical description of love, are like friends built on a rock. They do not crumble. They are friends in this life and the next.

So, the question always arises: How can one find and make valuable friends, soul friends, eternal, forever friends? The answer is both simple and complex. While the basics mentioned just above remain the same, examining friendship and friendship formation, one discovers that it differs with different ages and different stages.

The very young, little people, with an endless supply of time and little life experience, readily accept another little person as a friend, unless that little person is a toy destroyer or bites or something equally disagreeable. My three-year-old granddaughter, a happy, gregarious little girl, seems to make friends wherever she goes. It's in her nature. Once on a trip to Paris when she was just two and still in a stroller, she would speak to people on the street with a smile and a *bonjour*. Parisians don't customarily speak to people on the street, but many spoke to her. At home, in the church coffee hour when after a time there are few other children, she will circulate the room, standing patiently in the midst of a group of adults until they turn to her. She will then offer some exciting information about a new toy or a new hair bow. People are amazed and charmed.

Now she has a Monday/Friday alternating playdate with a little girl who is the child of her mother's college friend. At this writing, my grand-daughter has been doing this for about three weeks. The other day she said to her mother, "Rebecca [not her real name] is my best friend, Mommy."

My daughter repeated this to me with her own comment, "They could be lifelong friends."

My response? "Of course they could be." It happens. People who grow up on the same block marry one another. One of our sons married our daughter's best friend from growing up. It happens. These two little girls could be lifelong friends.

What will determine that is whether they each develop in character to be those who exhibit the qualities requisite for true friendship—which are much more than regular association. Will they grow in character develop-ment into fine young women? Will they grow in faith? Will they, along the way of growing up, not do irreparable harm to one another in speech or conduct? Could they be lifelong friends? Yes. One hopes so. One could encourage growth in the qualities that build friendships. All these things could be done. Still, these encouragements will have to be received and embraced by those little girls. So, the truth is, we'll have to wait and see. Time will tell.

Even with little ones with new emerging personalities and relation-ships, time wades in as the great revealer. In this age of instant everything, friendships are anything but. Which may be why it is reported that while surveyed adults could identify three good friends twenty years ago, sur-veyed adults today identify only two.[2] Just to be clear, here I'm not neces-sarily talking about soul friends, but good friends valuable in their lives.

It seems to be part of the reported current milieu or current charac-terization that preteen and teen girls are fickle, gossipy, sometimes viciously harmful, disrespectful of parents, smart mouthed, entitled, promiscuous, materialistic, faithless, and cliquey. Teenage boys, the current version goes, are all of these things and more, reckless and violent. Is this true? It is for multiple teens and their families. One of my friend's daughters, age fifteen, a lovely, accomplished Christian girl, a musician, has had multiple

---

2. See Rubin, *Happiness Project*, 142; and Powell, "Friendship," 137.

encounters with teens whose mouths are full of obscenities and whose disrespect for others can make one shudder.

However, to be fair, it is not true for other families and their teenagers. For example, I know a fifteen-year-old teenage girl who is a picture of loveliness, bright, fresh faced, a straight-A student, an accomplished soccer player, a chaplain in her eighth grade class last year, who just started high school and has a group of good friends, nine of whom have been together for years at their Christian school. Her brother, seventeen years old, who has been driving just a year, is an accomplished golfer who recently won a beautiful trophy for a current golf tournament in Los Angeles. Two years ago, he had the lead in the eighth grade class musical. He, too, is a straight-A student in a Christian high school. He, too, has a group of friends that he has had since first grade. Good kids. Ambitious, caring, and hopeful with what appear to be consistent, quality friendships. All of these friends were met in school. Could they be lifelong friendships? Very possibly. In fact, for them, in their short years, they already are lifelong friendships. Whether they develop into Christian soul friends will be determined by how they grow and mature in their Christian faith. I pray that for them.

My own research seems to indicate that a very high percentage of adults who report close friendships indicate that at least one of their closest friends is from school. My guess is that if you think of your closest friends, many of you will realize that at least one of them is from your school growing up.

Now we come to fully mature adult friendships, how to make them and how to maintain them. As you might imagine, this is more complicated. More moving pieces in one's life. More to protect. More to gain. More to lose. More to challenge. More limitations on time.

Our friend Aelred of Rievaulx, whom I mentioned early in the first chapter, is a good guide on the matter of forming and nurturing friendships. Aelred was a young courtier who became a young monk in the monastery of Rievaulx in northern England. Possessed of a fine intelligence, a good education, and a keen social intelligence, he wrote the little book entitled *Spiritual Friendship* in the 1100s. It has been a key work on Christian friendship ever since.

Aelred sees friendship formation as progressing in a series of stages. Describing the first stage, he points out quite rightly that there are naturally some people to whom we are particularly drawn. We want to meet them, to know them. We are interested, perhaps curious, engaged. Something about them attracts us, either personally or in their sharing a common interest with us. Maybe we met them at a class or a concert or at church or at the playground with the kids. This shared interest may be a clue, Aelred tells us, that this person could be someone with whom a friendship might develop. This is a stage that Aelred calls selection (connection). We would say today that we met so-and-so at some sort of a gathering, social or academic or work or church, and thought we would like to see about developing a relationship with them. It's some sort of connection. It's not a big thing. It's a clue. We make plans to get together for coffee or to meet in the park while our kids play or get out of the office briefly and grab a quick lunch together.

The next stage, which Aelred calls probation, admittedly not a term our modern ears are fond of, so perhaps we could think of it as a testing-the-water stage, can be a very long and extended period. This is the time when it is determined that both parties would like to develop a friendship. That is never actually said. It is tentatively understood. There is an initial invitation to do something. The other accepts. The time is spent pleasantly. Another invitation is extended by the second party and accepted, and the time is spent pleasantly. In the midst of this, slowly and carefully, individual preferences are shared about one thing or another, feelings are broached a bit, over time, personal concerns may surface. Over a significant period of time, one may turn to the other for counsel, for help, for encouragement. Little by little, easy does it, a friendship that is more than just getting together but includes some of the deep things of heart and soul and life, that sort of friendship begins to take root.

But time, taking time, is always on your side when treading cautiously, gently, lovingly in the territory of another's heart and soul. Barging in, no matter how well meaning, will feel like an unwanted intrusion. Advice, direction, demands, instructions should be avoided in most circumstances, if at all possible. These are cautions for both parties of an emerging friendship. Most adults understand that there is a sort of testing the water going on here. Unconsciously, for the most part, testing the relationship becomes more and more part of the discovery pattern of building the friendship. Questions that begin to develop are: Can I trust this new friend if I share a confidence? What does this friend say about others? Are they kind? How does this friend describe other relationships of family or other friends? Are they loving? When this new friend makes a date, is it kept? Are they dependable? What about the use of language, the use of resources? When you are with them, are you blessed or disheartened? Does your new friend respect your personal privacy, your space, your time, your priorities, your other friends and family members? Is this someone who speaks sincerely and truly about their love of Christ? None of these questions is answered in a week, or a month, or even a year. Time proves these things.

Aelred points out that "a foundation for friendship should be laid in the love of God."[3]

Growing friendships should always be tested for four character strengths:

- Loyalty: A truly loyal friend sees nothing in his friend but his heart.[4]

- Right intentions: Your friend has not entered into the friendship with you because of hope of any personal gain except your friendship and pleasing God.

- Discretion: A friend's conduct at all times is appropriate to a godly friendship.

- Patience: Your friend exhibits a personal willingness to receive constructive counsel and to bear a friend's burden.

If all of these concerns are satisfied, after some time, there comes a confirmation within oneself that this is a person to be trusted, and someone of increasing value in one's life. I think of this as the beginning of the confirmation of the Holy Spirit, and it usually is. With one caveat: it has to be said that sometimes our own human spirit can become so engaged that warnings that come from the Holy Spirit seem unimportant and go unnoticed. That is the risk of extending oneself in friendship. Nevertheless, even in times when it turns out to be a poor choice, friendship itself is still worth it. The nine out of ten times that you choose well more than make up for a faulty judgment here or there.

Aelred's third stage is the stage of admission. This is the beginning of a complete embracing of your new friend. There is much more association, much more sharing, much more genuine affection.

Finally, Aelred's fourth stage is the stage of soul friend. Now the friendship exists without qualification. We think of this as the stage of fully embracing our friend into our life. We no longer feel guarded in what we say or appropriately share with them. We include them in all sorts of other aspects of our lives. Some friends take vacations together, their kids play

---

3. Aelred of Rievaulx, *Spiritual Friendship*, 104.

4. Aelred of Rievaulx, *Spiritual Friendship*, 106.

together, get season tickets together, share meals regularly together, join the same car pools together, share life together regularly, pray together. It is, literally, a mutual embrace of another into the dearest areas of one's life. It is one of the most satisfying and fulfilling aspects of human life.

Cicero writes: "Without friends absolutely no life can be happy."[5]

And so we see the natural, thoughtful progression of a Christian soul friendship relationship. In all of this, time is of the essence, and almost always proves to be your ally. But not always.

In my research, I discovered that about a quarter of the folks I interviewed had experienced some sort of serious betrayal of a friend, and it wasn't uncommon for it to have been a long-term friend. It is one of the greatest shocks and personal harms that one can experience.

This is probably something we should discuss here, even though it can be painful.

Just as there is the element of unpredictability in life, there is an element of unpredictability in friendship. There are so many aspects at work in a person's life, so many different influences; and even knowing someone as well as one knows a close friend, there are still things that are too intimate to be shared, things that are confidences of others that must not be revealed, and pressures and intrusions of others' opinions that can be influential. To put it simply, people can change in their affections. After years of friendship, I find it hard to believe, even though I have seen it firsthand myself.

There is a passage in Scripture in Matt 18 that tells us that if someone wrongs us, we should go to that person and talk to them privately. When this results in reconciliation, all is restored. When it does not result in restoration, there are other more public steps suggested, but honestly, in my experience, I have never seen them be effective in today's church. Usually it feels like a stalemate.

Nevertheless, I discovered that we can learn about friendships even from those we have loved in Christ who choose other friends or turn against us by hurtful action. First of all, we can remember that Jesus, our Lord, had a betrayer friend among the original twelve disciples he chose. If that happened to Jesus, why should I be so surprised? I reasoned. In addition, I discovered that even with the complete cessation of the friendship, I still loved my old friend—even though I understood that she no longer wanted my friendship. I remembered all the good that I had received from

5. Cicero, as quoted in Aelred of Rievaulx, *Spiritual Friendship*, 110.

her over the years and all the joy we had shared, and I decided not to forget that either.

In the midst of this sorting out, I came across a prayer in one of my books that was a prayer for friends whose relationship was broken. The prayer rehearsed the remembrances of the sweet times the author had shared with his friend, the spiritual sharing they had done, the blessings of one another's lives that had taken place. This prayer was perfect for my situation. Later, in my research, I discovered that spiritual thinkers deal with this subject by maintaining that the love for a friend never dies completely. The loss of the friendship is a sorrow, because presumably the friendship will not be regained, but the memories of the blessings remain. It helped me.

With stories like this, you may wonder why anyone would want to venture to be a friend or why I would be so keenly in favor of highlighting it as a great benefit. We may wonder to ourselves if we are better off keeping free of friendship. One only wonders this until one remembers that "friendship is the unappreciated part of the spiritual life"[6] that brings us closer to God in Christ.

It is in the friendship relationship that I have the great joy and the great challenge to grow as a person, to seek to be conformed to the image of Christ, to learn the importance of the exercise of the fruits of the Spirit—love, joy, peace, patience, kindness, goodness, faithfulness, gentleness, and self-control (Gal 5:22)—in my own life. Indeed, outside of one's own family, it is only in friendship that we can learn to love our neighbors as ourselves. These things don't happen hypothetically, and we don't experience them by someone telling us about them. No. In our own personal lives, the closest we can be in demonstrating God's love is to be faithful in marriage (if married), faithful with our parents and our children and other family, and faithful in friendship. Our spiritual development and well-being depend on it. We must not forget that our soul friends on earth will be our blessed friends in eternity.

There can be no doubt. Friendship is transformative for our soul's good. Our very souls are being formed in it. It is a gift in this life and the next. As we engage in it more and more, we find it is an important part of our developing spiritual lives. Knowing this to be true, let us encourage one another to take time in our lives to engage in Christian friendship.

The Greek language has two words for time, *chronos*, clock time, chronometer time, ordinary, daily, earthly time as we know it, and *kairos*,

---

6. Martin, *Jesuit Guide*, 230.

eternal time, God's time, when things in this life and the next take place as God's ideal will ordained. In this life, our *chronos* leads to blessings in our *kairos*. To take time in this life for friends has an eternal blessing and heavenly reward.

5

The Invitation

ANNIE DILLARD, THE PULTIZER Prize–winning writer and Christian think-
er, once wrote: "How we spend our days is, of course, how we spend our
lives."[1]

I would add: how we spend our lives determines how we spend our
eternity. Are we human beings, souls, who have sought to grow into the
love of God? Have we welcomed the Lordship of Christ into our lives and
lived that out in the world? Have we received and accepted the guidance of
the Holy Spirit? Have we loved our neighbor?

There's an old story about a man who was an important business person, prominent in his community, who enjoyed much success in his life and
a maintenance person who worked in his building. It seems, according to
this story, that they both died on the same day. St. Peter warmly welcomed
the maintenance man and showed him to the place prepared for him. It
was a large mansion, beautiful, full of flowers and music, and the joyous
presence of those believers whom he had loved who had gone before him.

Then St. Peter showed the important man to the place prepared for
him. It was simple, unadorned, small and drab, and without company. The
man turned to St. Peter and said, "I just saw the place prepared for my
maintenance man. You can't be serious that this humble place is to be mine.
There must be some sort of mistake."

---

1. Dillard, *Writing Life*, 32.

St. Peter turned to him, "Unfortunately, this is not a mistake. I know you are disappointed, and I am sorry, but we can build up here only with the materials you send to us."

Our days, our lives, our eternity are all connected. You take you with you into eternity, and there you find many of the dear friends of faith with whom you have spent your days. Oh, I am not in any way negating that we are saved by grace through faith or that we don't flourish in heaven. Even those who are limited in such a way physically or mentally that they are unable to engage in or sustain friendship in this life can expect to be restored and fulfilled in eternity. Rather I am suggesting that heavenly existence is enriched by the person we are, the soul we become, and the Christian friends dear to our hearts who have gone before us and who welcome us. The question is: Do you want to arrive at the heavenly gates by the skin of your teeth, grateful beyond words, yes, but full of regret for much of your days and desperately alone; or do you want to arrive with a deep sense of joy and fulfilment and gratefulness to God for how God has blessed you with the cherished relationships of Christian soul friends that continue into eternity?

Cultivating friendships is one of the most important things we can do as we spend our days. It is through sincere, loving, spiritual friendship that we deepen into our spiritual lives. This is because friendship, real spiritual friendship, is challenging. With a Christian friend, we learn little by little, day by day, to grow in the joy of celebrating another, one who is not ourselves.

With a Christian friend, we are given a window into another Christian soul and the remarkable perspective of another's love of God. We learn, and we are deepened ourselves. With a Christian friend, we are required to grow in the fruits of the Spirit—love, joy, peace, patience, kindness, goodness, faithfulness, gentleness, and self-control (Gal 5:22)—without which a long-term soul friendship cannot survive. With a Christian friend, we learn forgiveness and self-sacrifice, if we want to keep a cherished friendship over time. With a Christian friend, we grow and develop more and more into the mature soul God intends for us to be.

In Protestant Christian spiritual formation, it is a maxim that to grow, we take time to study Scripture, time for regular worship and communion in community, and time to pray. I would suggest that to grow in Christ there is another spiritual discipline we have long neglected, spiritual friendship.

If we neglect friendship, we may find ourselves having neglected one of the key spiritual avenues leading to our eternal life. When we neglect friendships, we neglect not only the potential blessing of another, but we neglect our own blessing in this life and the next.

If cherishing friendship is so important for our spiritual lives, it makes sense for us to consider how to cultivate these relationships that have the potential to be a blessing beyond measure. When we were very young, probably most of us thought that making friends and keeping them was easy. Nothing to think about too much.

Most of us start out fairly oblivious to potential complications.

If you have come from a loving and accepting family—even if you have rather pesky older siblings—you still probably have believed that making friends was as easy as pie. You just show up, smile, talk a bit, and presto chango, you've got a new friend. We think this, because it is, generally speaking, the way people begin to make friends, and it comes to us instinctively. Lots of us experience this in childhood. Let me describe an experience from my own childhood that is nothing remarkable at all, but it will make the point. If you think back to your childhood, you may have had a similar experience.

The time I'm remembering is when I was four years old. I was wearing a nicely starched and ironed dress with a big bow tied in the back. (Little girls dressed this way in the early 1950s.) It was a beautiful, sunshiny day in Cincinnati, Ohio, in the Hyde Park district. My young parents had rented an upper-floor apartment in a brick corner building at the end of the street. I remember the apartment had big, red cabbage roses on the dining room wallpaper. The street we lived on, Victoria Avenue, was, to my memory, a street that ran up a rather large hill. The sidewalk lay up and down the street on either side. I decided that I would take my tricycle and ride up and down the sidewalk and find a friend. Believe it or not, this was safe those many years ago. So, out the door I went and began peddling up the hill on my friendship quest.

It wasn't long before I was nearing the top of the hill, and there to my right I saw two kids who looked to be just about my age. I stopped and got off my bike and walked up the driveway to them. "Hi," I said, "I'm Pam. Do you want to be friends?"

They nodded. "I'm Mary," the older one said, "and he is Peter," she said, pointing to her younger brother.

Then the three of us squeezed our little bodies into the narrow window well that peeked upon their driveway, our knees nearly touching our chins, and talked about what we could play. With that simple question, that important invitation—do you want to be friends?—we became friends.

After that day, we played together often. We ate dinner at one another's dining tables. When my father was transferred a few years later and we left the city, we still kept in touch. Whenever we returned to Cincinnati, I would visit them. As young teens, I remember at least once spending the night at their house. Not surprisingly, the distance between us grew, and the last contact I had with them was wedding gifts exchanged. Nevertheless, my affectionate memory remains for these two dear little friends of my early childhood.

Just how deep a friendship was this, you might ask. Surely as four-year-olds and even as twelve-year-olds there wasn't much that lasted here. To a certain extent you would be correct. We no longer have any contact with one another. I have no idea where either of them is, and I have never tried to find them, although I have wondered about it. So one could deduce that the value was in the children's friendship, the joy of companionship, playing together. Childhood friendships could be characterized, generally speaking, as just that. A significant portion of these friendships do not go beyond that—especially if one or both parties move away. It's no surprise, considering the transient nature of society today, that many childhood friendships don't translate into mature friendships.

What has surprised me in the research I have done with a questionnaire of close to one hundred Christian adults is that many people report that a childhood friend did materialize into a lifelong mature friend. This usually means that they have remained in the same community growing up. Certainly, this outcome requires all sorts of variables to correspond. At least initially, parents have to be willing to facilitate the meetings of little friends. Of course, mature friends have to have more in common than knowing each other since childhood. Mature friends have to have some particular interests and values in common as adults. Mature friends usually experience a profound resonance with one another. Mature friends generally share lifestyles that correspond in significant ways, and there has to be some sort of regular contact that maintains the relationship satisfactorily for each friend. Even if you have childhood friends, dear to your heart, who continue in life and become adult friends, the truth is that either consciously or subconsciously, at some point, you have chosen one another again as adult friends. If both friends are Christians, I believe that the Holy Spirit was there providing the glue.

A few years ago, I was at a garden wedding that my husband was performing. It was intimate, family and a very few friends. After the wedding, sitting on the brick patio enjoying the lush summer breeze that kisses San Diego and surrounded by the profusion of flowers of a master gardener, we were all chatting while munching on sandwiches and cookies and sipping lemonade or champagne. It was a happy day, a blessed day of acknowledging the goodness of God. Just two years before, my husband and I had rushed to this home where one of our dearest friends, Hugh (not his real name), had dropped dead from a massive heart attack. Now, his widow, Mary (not her real name), had met another love for her life. In retirement, they were going to journey together and celebrate their remaining years together.

Perhaps you've been in these situations yourself. Times when all seems right with the world when in recent memory all seemed wrong. Once again, God was drawing blessing out of brokenness. We were the witnesses.

As we sat there with the groom, others gathered around us. One man, John, a successful businessman, and his wife, faithful church members, were there. Old stories began to surface amid much laughter and teasing.

Then, to my surprise, the groom said jovially to John, "I remember when we first met."

I thought that was probably recently. Since he was there with his wife, I assumed it was his wife who was connected to the bride. What followed surprised me.

John laughed, "Yes, that day at the elementary school."

Then Mark, the groom, pointing to John and taking us all into the conversation with his eyes, said: "This guy—this guy—you should have seen him. It was the third grade and . . ."

"And I was brand new at the school," John tried to interrupt.

But the groom was not to be interrupted, "And it was the first day and he came in the back door, the wrong door of the classroom near the cloakroom, and I was hanging up my coat. He looked pretty scared."

"Well," said John, not to be intimidated, "he"—and here John pointed to the groom—"he was the first person I saw."

Everyone laughed.

"The first person," the groom emphasized, smiling, "And John said to me: 'Do you want to be my friend?' And I said, 'Yes!' And we've been friends ever since."

I had a sharp intake of breath. Wow! That's decades, I thought. They've been retired for some years. I didn't want to miss this opportunity to ask a probing key question.

"So, have you been connected ever since then? Have you been in the same community all these years? Have you stayed in touch?"

"Oh, absolutely!" They both nodded and went on to elaborate all the various things they had done together as young men and men with families and on and on and on.

"Really?" Maybe you're saying to yourself. "Just in the cloakroom when you're eight years old? Is it that simple?"

Well, it can be, and the surprising truth is that it often is—just that simple.

So here is the first key to unlocking the mystery of how to make friends: the invitation.

There is something about the invitation to the right person that is a bit like open arms. To the right person, who themselves may have been desiring or are receptive to a friendship, the invitation is an open door if there ever was one. This happens at all ages and all stages.

An important reminder is that there is no statute of limitations in your life that dictates it is too late to find friends. And there is no statute of limitations on the invitation.

There is no doubt that the practice and the positive experience of making friends as children has the potential to provide a baseline for a lifetime. The experiences I have just recounted were certainly formative. Beyond the fact that they were happy, positive experiences, unknowingly, we had all hit upon a key aspect, an initial step, in developing relationships. The invitation: "Do you want to be friends?" The invitation comes in all sorts of forms, but at its heart it is always this question in one form or another. Still we all know that it's never just the invitation. It's never just that easy, is it? Dig deeper, and one finds that there is always a preliminary requirement. Let me ask you: Do you want to issue an invitation? Well, then, you have to venture out, extend yourself. True, sometimes this is easy, natural and routine.

However, before anyone invites anyone anywhere, he or she has to admit either consciously or unconsciously to that God-given yearning for relational connection. Usually, one doesn't think about that at all. Usually, it is thought of simply as just a good idea—a lighthearted idea. "I think I'll invite a few good friends to go to the movies!" There are some recognizable strengths in this idea. The person is thinking of something pleasurable that their friends would like, and the person is considering inviting tried-and-true good friends. This is not the sort of invitation that requires the average person to extend themselves that much. This is a happy idea. A safe bet. It will work out that everyone can come or not—but it won't make or break anyone's heart. There are too many stable elements in place.

It's the simplest and the sweetest sort of invitation—like the four-year-old on the trike asking two other little ones: Do you want to be friends? Or the scared third grade boy in a new school who blurts out to the first boy he sees, "Do you want to be my friend?" Or a group of longtime friends who enjoy movies together.

These happy, simple invitations are just the beginning of what it means to consider the world of invitations. So, let's consider that for a while. There is the formal "You will accept" invitation. That's the invitation from your boss to the Christmas party. It's the invitation from your faculty department head to attend an event. As a young Air Force officer's wife, I remember receiving an invitation to coffee from the general's wife. The wording was such that there was no question but that "yes, ma'am, I will be happy to attend" was the reply. Most of us have received the beautifully scripted wedding invitation with the enclosed reply card worded: "We will attend/ We regret we will be unable to attend." We mark the appropriate line, sign, send, and, hopefully, attend.

The invitation is a key part of social interaction and community building. It is in these most formal expressions and the vast bridge that extends between children's play dates and wedding receptions that we gather as neighbors, associates, colleagues, community members, members of particular social groups, neighborhoods, school populations, church fellowships, work groups, sports teams, bridge clubs, quilting groups, prayer groups, covenant groups, volunteers and religious communities, church small groups, family dinners and reunions, and, finally, individual friends. Somewhere in the mix of these gatherings—before anything started—someone decided to issue an invitation. These invitations come in personal face-to-face conversation, by word of mouth, in the mail, by phone, by text, by email, and by all sorts of other means; but however they are issued, they come from an idea that someone had a desire at one time to gather with others. Behind any and all of these invitations, there is, in some sort of way, initially, an individual who is reaching out for community.

A key thing to remember is that invitations are personal.

"Well, not really," you may say. "Not when five hundred people are invited."

I have to reply, "Don't count on it." Someone in the mix is noticing and hoping for each one to attend. That is why the wise person does not ignore the importance of the invitation when building a life in community and hoping to form a meaningful life of friendship.

Once I received a typed letter, hand signed, from a friend I had known for years. Always a gifted leader, over the course of his lifetime, he had become a very important person with an esteemed position and entourage of assistants and notable multiple speaking and social events. Although the letter was personal and invitational in nature, I ignored it. I thought, "Oh, that's nice to be included in this mass mailing his assistant has done for him." I didn't think a thing about it after that.

A few years later in a conversation with that friend, he mentioned his letter.

"Oh, yes," I responded genuinely, "I did get your letter about that and I so appreciated being included. Very thoughtful of you since you know I am interested in that topic."

"Why didn't you respond?" he asked quietly.

I was surprised at the question. "Oh," I replied, "isn't that just like you to include me along with your five hundred other friends?" and I laughed.

"It wasn't like that, "he said. "It was just a small group. Less than a dozen."

I was surprised and disappointed in myself. Of course, I apologized, and of course, this friend accepted that apology, and our conversation and our friendship continued unabated. Nevertheless, I have thought of that unaccepted invitation many times since, and regretted my nonchalance. Invitations are always personal. You may not think they are, but they are personal. To someone. Somehow. Always.

Jesus, understanding the great need of human beings to be connected issued a multitude of invitations. He gathered a group of friends around him with an invitation, "Come. Follow me." Jesus invited the children to join with him and refused to keep them away. He not only welcomed them, he blessed them (Mark 10:13–16). When Zacchaeus was perched in the tree, Jesus looked up, saw him and invited himself to dinner at Zacchaeus's house (Luke 19:1–10). Salvation came to that house that day, because Zacchaeus joyfully accepted that invitation. Zacchaeus was blessed, and indeed his whole community was blessed because of his vow to return monies he had cheated away from others. One heartbreaking invitation occurred when Jesus invited the rich young ruler to follow him. The text says that Jesus, looking at him, loved him. Yet the young wealthy man couldn't imagine a life without his wealth, and "he went away sorrowing" (Luke 18:18–23).

Jesus invited Peter, James, and John to join him as he climbed the Mount of Transfiguration (Matt 17:1–9). They accepted his invitation, and Jesus gave them the opportunity to witness one of the greatest spiritual revelations recorded. Indeed all of Jesus's life was an invitation to recognize him as the Son of God who came to bring blessing, hope, and redemption to all who believed and followed him.

The best of all is the wonderful revelation of the apostle John who, in the Spirit, envisions Jesus standing at the door of the heart and knocking—asking, inviting himself to come in and be with that soul. The invitation continues throughout our lives. Jesus invites himself to be with us, with you, with me. God with us. Immanuel. So, we pause and reflect as we realize that some invitations have a spiritual destination, even if at the time they may seem ordinary.

I will always cherish the memory of a simple letter of invitation that I received when I was pastoring an African American church. I was just beginning the pastorate at that church when this letter arrived from the local elementary school principal. It was addressed to all the clergy in that particular area of the city, which was a black area. The letter began, "Dear Black Pastor." I confess that it startled me at first, since I am a white woman, but at that point I was still becoming accustomed to my new context. The letter was an invitation to attend a meeting at the local elementary school. The meeting was to include clergy and the elementary school teachers and administration. The meeting was to be held the next week. I wasn't at all sure how this would be or if I could even reasonably have a voice in the community into which I had just recently entered. Still I prayed, and gratefully, I went.

The gathering was held in a meeting room—just the right size for what I would estimate now as about twelve to sixteen teachers and administrators and eight or nine clergy. Somewhere around twenty to twenty-five of us. The principal led the meeting, welcoming us and asking us to introduce ourselves. Then, the principal explained why she had asked for this meeting. "Our kids are being recruited into gangs," she said. "We need the help of the community to combat this." Then, one by one each teacher spoke about his or her classroom and what they were seeing happening to the kids. Children as young as third grade were being recruited.

"What could they do?" we asked.

"They're spotters for drug dealers," the teachers replied.

The anguish on the teachers' faces was unmistakable. The sixth-grade teacher told how he could now look out on the playground and tell which kids were gang related, because they were wearing expensive athletic shoes or they had new bikes. The plea was, "Can you help us? What can we do to save these children?" Everyone expressed concern, the kind of concern that one expresses faced with helplessness. It seemed impossible.

I went back to the church with a heavy heart. What could be done to help these children, to shield them from the drug epidemic that had destroyed so many—including some of the lives of my own congregational members? The next week the session of the church met. The session is the governing body of a Presbyterian church. There were six elder members. The pastor is always the moderator. I told them about the meeting at the school and what the teachers were reporting. I told them about the shoes and wished aloud that our little, twenty-one-member poor church had the money to supply shoes to those children for doing the right things. It seemed hopeless. The elders shook their heads in sorrow at what seemed like the inevitable epidemic coming to our community.

Then one of the elders, Betty Iles (her real name), said: "We should pray." One by one each head bowed, and one by one each prayed a heartfelt prayer for the children and asked God for direction in what we should do. So far as I could tell, no one had any realistic idea of anything we could do.

After some time, Betty raised her head and said, "We should start supplying the shoes to deserving kids. We should do it."

Everyone sighed. How would we afford it? I had already done the numbers. I told them we would need about $5,000 in order to award three kids (the best athlete, the best citizen, the best student) in each classroom each term a pair of shoes of their choosing. "I have never raised that amount of money. I don't know where it would come from," I said. The session decided to go ahead. We contacted the school to tell them what we proposed.

They loved the idea, but the question came back to us, "Can you afford this?"

The elders replied, "We can with God's help."

Well, you can probably guess how this story unfolds. It was the most remarkable, astonishing really, thing that I ever had happen in my pastoral ministry. As soon as the word got around that we were raising money for the kids, money started pouring in. The shoes endeavor was written up in the local paper. We received two small grants. A check arrived from Italy, of all places, for $750. "Keep on helping those kids," the note read.

At the end of the first semester when the teachers awarded their three outstanding kids in their classrooms at a school assembly, the church had received $5,000. When the winners of those awards were announced, they seemed to glow with joy. God blessed the faith of that little twenty-one-member congregation who accepted an invitation to reach out and help. Because of that, many were blessed over the years.

There is so much more to this story, but of all the letters of thanks the church received over those two years from student winners in three elementary schools (we adopted three), one letter from a little fourth grade boy written in an uneven script touched me the most. It said:

> Dear Pastor Pam and Messiah Church, Thank you for my shoes. They are awesome! When my brother was shot last year, I was so sad he was gone. I thought that I would probably be shot too. But now that I have won the shoes, I think I have a chance to live! Signed: Derek [not his real name]

God blessed the faith of that little congregation, and because of that, many were blessed over the years. It's a Zacchaeus kind of story, I have thought; because he accepted an invitation, so many were blessed.

Here's the thing to remember: *Sometimes an invitation that is directed just to you, upon acceptance, turns out to be a blessing to a whole community.* In these cases, it always seems unexpected and astonishing. It's wonderful to see the Holy Spirit at work!

The fascinating thing about the invitation is that it can take a variety of multiple forms. We all recognize the question that frames the invite. Do you want to . . . do something? Even the youngest of children recognize that, but as we grow up and become more mature, invitations surface in multiple ways. A key to an enjoyable life of personal interactions requires one to recognize subtlety.

One such subtlety was revealed in the expression of affirmation from one person to another and the effect that expression may have. There is a little book in which the letters of the theologian Karl Barth and poet/artist Carl Zuckmayer are published. The book is entitled *A Late Friendship*. This friendship developed at the end of Barth's life and not far from the end of Zuckmayer's. As it all began, they were both recognized in their field.

They both had achieved prominence. Their friendship had its genesis in a little note that Barth wrote to Zuckmayer after Barth had read one of Zuckmayer's poems. It was not a let-me-get-to-know-you note. It was a simple note of appreciation and admiration for Zuckmayer's art well expressed. One could reasonably doubt that Barth expected a reply from his little note. Nevertheless, a reply he received, and a late friendship was ignited with the meeting of two minds and souls.

Over the course of the last two years of Barth's life, they corresponded with increasing personal expression, often opening their letters with "Dear Friend." Twice they visited one another—even though they resided in different countries and neither was spry. At a time in life when one may assume that neither man was looking for or needing another friendship, one invitation opened the doors of their hearts and stopped in for an extended chat, warmed by the fire of the soul. There's a tenderness in the correspondence that is intimate and caring, as well as the sparkle of great intellects. There is a faith shared as well. Reading this, it struck me that friendships emerge in all ages and stages of life, and one should never think that one's relational life is at a close. The joy of connecting, really connecting, with other like-minded souls never ends. It is singularly energetic. It seems that God has designed human beings in such a way that we are neither too young nor too old to make friends. Indeed, soul friendships are for eternity.

Something similar happened when J. R. R. Tolkien and C. S. Lewis became acquainted. They were colleagues with mutually recognized intellect and creativity, but one could not rightly call them friends. Perhaps we could have said they were social friends and colleagues. But then, Tolkien took a risk. He bundled up some of his writing and sent it to Lewis to see what he thought. Any writer would say that this was a huge risk of feeling exposed and perhaps humiliated. However, what resulted was a genuine meeting of the minds and hearts and souls of these two men. It materialized into a friendship that has blessed the entire Christian world with their writings and interactions.

On the same vein as examples of well-known people, there is the case of Thomas Jefferson and John Adams, longtime friends, family friends, and then after a split in their personal friendship over policy and politics, the friendship ended. However, later, when both were on their deathbeds, the physician and friend of each of these great men, Benjamin Rush, encouraged them to write to one another. They had shared so much over the years, the formation of the republic, their years as ambassadors in Europe,

Jefferson's warm affection for Adams's family, and the great sadness Adam's family felt over the loss of Jefferson's friendship. Rush encouraged them to write, to make peace with one another, to forgive one another, to be an example for others of God's gracious forgiveness. Trusting in their friend Rush, they began correspondence. As it turned out, they both died on the same day, July 4, 1826, fifty years to the day after the Declaration of Independence was signed. They had corresponded for the last couple of years of their lives, exchanging 150 letters before they died. When they died, they died as friends. All of this because of an invitation—an invitation to reach out, to forgive, and to restore a broken friendship.

It's almost impossible to predict what might happen when one willing heart reaches out to another. Yet, whereas it may seem to be almost impossible, it is always possible that the Holy Spirit will be at work, blessings will be far-reaching, and friendship or renewed friendship will result. When that happens, there is a kind of fresh joy in life.

6

Friendship in Groups

HUMAN BEINGS ARE SOCIAL animals. Throughout human history people have banded together in groups. There are all sorts of reasons for people grouping, survival being the chief among them. We may like to think that grouping for survival may have been true and necessary in the primitive past of the Bronze Age but is no longer necessary in these modern days.

The fact is that grouping for survival is going on today in multiple parts of the world. One of the most prominent modern examples that I personally knew of is that of the Lost Boys of Sudan. These were Christian boys from South Sudan who were being sought for capture by the Muslim fighters of North Sudan. They were taken from their families and incorporated into the armies of North Sudan. There were many political reasons for this invasion of the Christian south by the Muslim north, but primary was the fact that the south was oil rich, a resource that could provide wealth for those who controlled it.

The stories the different boys recounted were all the same although many came from different villages. Their village had been invaded. Their mothers and sisters often raped and killed. Their fathers executed before their eyes. Seeing this, the boys who could escape did. They fled with such terror that they literally ran out of Sudan. In fact, they walked across the wide span of Africa to escape. As they walked they became connected with other boys with the same story. Older boys took care of younger boys. They banded together for comfort and protection. They prayed together.

No doubt they wept together. They were friends. Leaders emerged among them. They were no longer isolated. They were in a group. Eventually, they were a large group of refugees. Recognized by the UN, they were taken in groups and resettled in various nations around the world.

Here is where my experience intersects with theirs. I remember well when a group of the Lost Boys arrived in Pittsburgh, Pennsylvania. It was 2001, I was on the faculty of Trinity Episcopal School for Ministry, an Episcopal seminary in the Anglican tradition. Trinity was located in Ambridge, a town on the outskirts of Pittsburgh proper. Encouraged by our colleague Grant LeMarquand, a former African missionary (now an Anglican bishop), several of us at the seminary gathered together in the basement of a local church to serve these newly arrived refugees one of the first dinners they had in the States. We provided a lot of food on a buffet table. We thought that these were tall, young men who had come out of terror and privation. They had to be hungry. They needed care and resettlement help and Christian community. Our goal was to be among the first of those who extended a welcoming hand.

They arrived, the Lost Boys, about eighteen to twenty of them, but as they walked in, it was surprisingly quiet. Not what one would expect from a group of teenage to twenty-something boys and men. They were led by an impressive and dominant African American woman who was in charge of their resettlement. She was a representative of the Anglican Church. She introduced herself and the group of boys to us. She knew them. Immediately one was aware that she was serving as a parental figure for them. It was impressive. For our part, we opened our arms to them in welcome. When they were seated, we prayed, and then we served them dinner. We piled the plates high with food. Chicken and potatoes and salad and rolls and all sorts of desserts. They ate carefully, sparingly, cautiously. Different food. A different country. A long flight. A massive change. A whole new world. Alien. In fact, they could not eat much—not having eaten much for years.

The food served, we sat interspersed among them. One of our guests that I sat with was a tall young man, about twenty-one years old. "I am Pam," I said to him. "What is your name?"

"I am Christopher," he said politely, softly.

"How old are you, Christopher?" I asked him.

"I'm not sure exactly," he said. I thought, so much has been lost to them, the things about life that a mother remembers. Christopher continued, "I think about twenty-one years."

I smiled at him, "Ah," I said," I have a son your age."

After some discussion about the circumstances of his finding out where his group would be resettled and the flight to America, and some explanation of what the various foods were on his plate, I asked him if he wanted to tell me his story. It helps in grief to tell one's story, but I wasn't sure if he would want to or not.

He stopped eating, and looked at me. "Yes," he said. "I would like to tell you." Then he began a tale of loss and sorrow that was almost beyond conceiving. "The soldiers came into my village with machetes and machine guns," he told me as his fork traced the food on the plate. "First they killed my father. Then, they took my mother and sisters." Here his voice trailed off. "And killed them," he said very softly.

My heart went out to him. I said all anyone could say, "I am so sorry this happened, Christopher, I am glad you were able to escape."

Then, remembering what I had told him about my own family and looking into my eyes, he said softly, "Will you be my mother?" I reached out and hugged him.

Later in the evening, the woman, the very impressive leader, whose name I wish I could remember, gathered the boys in a group in front of our tables. I realized that Christopher was swallowed up in that group. The leader, after some words of appreciation and orientation for us to the boys' situation, gave each boy an opportunity to share what his dreams were for his new life in America. Several of them chose to speak. I found my mind and heart distracted by Christopher. How would it be for him? Where would he find his life again? I came to myself as an impressive boy with a deep African voice identified himself as the spiritual leader of their group. Others nodded immediately. He carried a small, tattered Bible. He wanted to become a bishop. A few years later I discovered that he had indeed become a bishop. Then, there was one who wanted to become a doctor. He had been the one in their group who cared for the wounds of the others. Again, I found out later about him. He had not been able to accomplish his education. It was too much—the great horrors, the terrible escape, the long journey. Alone and terrified. His friends encouraged him, but his heart was too broken. Christopher did not speak.

Immediately at the end of their personal accounts, and what seemed fairly abrupt to me, their leader ushered them as a group from the front of our room out and into the waiting bus. I realized that they were on a schedule for their transportation. We were only able to call out our goodbyes.

"Farewell, Christopher," I said. "The Lord be with you." I never knew exactly what happened to him, and we were kept informed in only the most general way. I have thought of him many times and hoped for him.

Some things I do know are that the boys were settled four to six to an apartment. They became little families together—friends in the deepest sense of the word. They needed each other. Not now for physical safety but for emotional and spiritual stability. They were grouped together in hope for their new life. The church oversaw their resettlement. I am certain that few if any of them would have been able to survive those years without the benefit of the other boys. Once they had saved themselves. Then they saved one another. They had a group that was first a defense against danger from outside. Then, as the group developed into a group of friends, it became a defense against the challenges of the new life. It wasn't where they lived that mattered so much anymore. It was whom they were with. They had found a family with the other Lost Boys. Friends. A place to belong.

There is the fact that our circumstances in the Western world, in the church, are not even remotely to be compared with the terrible struggles of those Lost Boys. Yet one cannot minimize the growing reports of loneliness in our society, the fragmentation of families through divorce or separation, the chronic absence of fathers, the pervasive power of opioids to drain the life out of our neighbors and their children, the reality that there are our own sons and daughters disconnected and drifting on the streets of America, lost, the rampant gang killings in my own city, Chicago. One cannot ignore that there are abortions going on around us, and certainly in Chicago, where I live, there are kids who have seen their own parents killed before their eyes. Then there are those so steeped in affluence that they no longer consider life abundant but rather meaningless enough to end it themselves, and even in affluent areas in America, there is a notable population who are hungry. No, we are not fleeing from the terror of North Sudan. Many of us are fleeing from ourselves and the hollow, lonely disconnections in our lives.

Here, once again, the biblical truth is indisputable. God has said, as recounted in Gen 2, "It is not good for man to be alone." God has connected us into families because we all need a place to belong. We have the church as the family of God's people. A place to belong. Yet even in such a large institution as the church, we each must find our particular group, our own personal friends. Not acquaintances. Friends.

The church seeks to help people find the personal connection to others through providing the opportunity for small groups. The small group movement once again burst upon the American church scene in the 1970s, and as a young mom I remember organizing my home church's small groups for the Lenten season. Out of about 1000 church members, about 350 signed up to be in Lenten small groups. It had a huge impact on the congregation. People began to experience afresh the deep and personal interactive power of human relationships in Christ. People made new friends. Those who knew "everybody" became better friends. It provided connection that was real and personal. It enhanced people's lives. It enhanced people's spiritual lives. It strengthened that church.

There is something distinct about friendship in groups that provides another dimension in the friendship landscape.

As I survey my own life, I realize that I have been a part of many groups. Some of them not mentioned here are dear to me. However, I can think of three key groups over the years that have been essentially important friendship groups. They taught me the value of sharing spiritual life with others as a key way that God opens and broadens the scope of our souls.

So, I will probe with you the nature of those three groups. What will emerge are my own personal experience and development as an example of the power of friendship in groups.

The three groups I will characterize for the purpose of our consideration are quite different in initial stated purpose, size, and longevity. One couples' group of ten lasted two years. One women's group of nine lasted nine years, and one clergy group of forty is on its thirty-seventh year as I write this. Each group of Christian friends in its unique way has provided me a lifetime's worth of the deep joy of Christian fellowship and belonging. Each group was one of the major blessings of my personal life and spiritual development.

Friendship in groups and the opportunity to be in friendship groups is easily ignored or minimized by those of us living a hectic modern life. It's hard to find time, and that is not just a cliché. It is hard to find time. However, I believe that missing the experience of a group of friends committed to a spiritual friendship is missing a key part of the joy of being human and the opportunity to open oneself to unique engagements of the working of the Holy Spirit through the spiritual gifts, love, and grace of others. In short, friendship in groups provides an important avenue for spiritual growth and development.

The first small group that I was ever part of was a group my husband and I helped form, without realizing what an important endeavor it was. We were in our twenties, young Christians, fresh with just having read the New Testament for the first time. Without Bible commentaries or even being aware that there were Christian bookstores, we were eager to talk with others like us. We wanted to talk about the Bible, explore Scripture, understand.

But where to start? After his having served during the Viet Nam war as a hospital administrator, my husband and I were now returning to his home church in Indianapolis. Truly with only the briefest conversation between us—"Wouldn't it be great to get some others together to talk about the Bible?"—Sunday morning we began to invite other young couples we barely knew to join us. "Do you want to come to our house Friday night and talk about the Bible?" That's how it started. It must have been a divine appointment, because of the four couples we invited over the course of two Sundays, all four eagerly accepted. We were twenty-somethings, most of us young parents. We all had reasonably comparable backgrounds. We all had a reasonably comparable educational achievement. We were all motivated to study Scripture together. Here's a clue to the cohesiveness of this particular group. There were a lot of shared similar factors. Right from the beginning, these factors provided a personal sense of connectedness. Those elements don't necessarily ensure success in a group, but they can be good building blocks.

Excitement over our study every Friday night remained unabated for two years. None of us cancelled a Friday night that I can remember. We almost never missed attending except for sickness. We gathered with our Bibles. We talked. We laughed. We shared our lives. We studied the New Testament, taking turns leading, teaching one another. Then, we prayed. Oh, of course, you must be thinking, "Nice. A closing prayer." No. I'm not describing a three-minute closing prayer. We prayed, each one, out loud. We poured out our hearts to the Lord in the tenderness and the safety of that group. It wasn't unusual for us to pray together at closing for forty-five minutes or even more. That sort of prayer has impact. It is transformative. It probably wouldn't surprise you that many other young couples in the church became more committed Christians because of the testimony of that group. I still think of those two years with gratitude. I still today consider many of the members of that group as my dearest friends. We have walked through life together and still do, to my eternal gratitude.

Still, circumstances never stay the same, do they?

So much has happened to all of us in those forty-plus years since we met together so fervently. Did the destructive power of the culture and time passing get to us? Of course. I wouldn't have believed it at that time, but it did. Take a moment and think about the various life crises that the years can hold and you can imagine trauma of various kinds. Most especially and publicly there was a chronic debilitating disease that took the life of one of those dear friends just this last year. Yes, life took its toll. Nevertheless, all remained Christians and people committed in faith. Of the ten of us, three of us became Presbyterian pastors, and among the five couples' fourteen children, four of the children became pastors themselves and another a Presbyterian elder. All of our lives and the lives of our children were redirected, but was it perfect? No. Were there problems among us at different times? Yes. Did it all turn out to be perfect? Not exactly. It was, as I like to characterize it, real life. The naïve idea that Christian friendship makes everything smooth is just not the way life in this world develops. But along with a loving marriage and family, Christian friendships certainly make life worth living and heaven worth anticipating. Christian friendship is one of the top three or four aspects of life that make life truly joyful. Without deep spiritual friendships our souls are shuttered off from eternal joys of life and soul.

I confess that whenever I think of small groups, or teach on small groups, or lead a small group, this group of ten, these dear friends in Christ, these ten, are never far out of my mind. Of all the Bible studies, seminary classes, and lectures I have ever heard or myself given, nothing was as educative and formative as those two years when the ten of us sat on the floor with our Bibles in our laps and together studied the Bible and prayed.

Since then, I have experienced, as perhaps you have too, all sorts of groups. There are dinner groups, luncheon groups, women's groups, men's groups, professional groups, and parents' groups. There are couples groups and singles groups, music groups and study groups, and bridge groups. There are tennis groups, symphony groups, or Art League groups. There are yoga groups, and mediation and mindfulness groups, and grief groups. There are alum groups and reunion groups, to name just a fraction of the kinds of groups that are available. The value of these groups arises from the common interest, the opportunity to share or socialize, the associative value of making new friends for personal or emotional support, and the opportunity to learn and grow. They all can be good, enriching, enjoyable, and important in a life. The fact is that groups of human beings getting together to share a healthy aspect of life can almost always be positive.

The theological truth always stands (whether people are believers or not): God made us for one another and our lives are richer when that is realized.

There was a time in my life that felt as if I were in a sea of isolation. In fact, I wasn't, but that is how it felt. We had moved to a new city where my husband had been called as a pastor of a large Presbyterian church. I had left my faculty position in Pennsylvania, and as if that weren't enough, I experienced a health crisis, hospitalization, and required bed rest for some weeks. People in the church were kind, of course, but I myself felt adrift. Then, one of the women in the church, a rather marvelous, accomplished woman who was always doing good, said to me: "What we need to do is to form a group. How does that sound?"

"Good," I said somewhat wearily and yet hopefully.

"Let's make a list of women. We could meet for six weeks and do a Bible study," she said.

Within a couple of months, the group gathered. Nine women total, and to my delight, they were all very happy about forming a group. What was especially interesting about this group was that it was a group that spanned different ages. There was about twenty-five years between the oldest and the youngest woman in the group. Nevertheless, all wanted to be together and all wanted to grow in spiritual friendship. And so it started, this six-week group that after six weeks renegotiated for another six weeks, and then another and another. For nearly nine years we met. For years, we did strictly Bible study, personal sharing, and prayer. A few times, we read a Christian book together and discussed it. We began to have the group to our homes for lunch, which was pleasant for a while and then grew to be too much. We returned to morning coffee and sweet rolls and fruit. We grew into a deep friendship that often included spouses, as we celebrated birthdays and all sorts of dinners together for all sorts of reasons. Since we were in San Diego where the weather was almost always beautiful, we would often sit on a deck in the sunlight with the sun playing on the sparkling water, and we would share our lives and our prayer concerns. We prayed for one another, our husbands, our children, our grandchildren, our church. We worshipped together on Sundays and felt a deep refreshment in sharing worship together. Now, I look back on that group that spanned most of our life in San Diego, and I find much joy in the recollections of those friendships in Christ and what they meant to me in that time of life—for they were an embodiment of community, of faith, and of much happiness.

But it wasn't perfect. Just to mention a few of the matters that emerged. The first six weeks, the woman whose idea it had been to form the group for six weeks was on to another good work. One woman went through a crisis that seemed irrevocably serious. We were all terribly grieved. She considered dropping out, but we held onto her. In faith, not only she survived, but her family too. Happily, they are all thriving now to a greater extent than before. Yet again, time takes its toll. During the course of nearly a decade, people age and people and their life circumstances change. Nine years is an uncommonly long time of survival for a small group, and I have often been grateful for those women and their friendship in Christ.

Nevertheless, you may be asking yourself, how could the group conclude when the group was such a pure delight—a real joy for so many years, and why would it be used it as an example? I used it as an example to make an important point. Yes, it was a delight for that time, but in time, people change and with that change comes a change in the small group. Small groups aren't perfect, and when members experience other significant demands in their lives, it affects the group. And then there is the very human tendency/temptation to be critical of one another. Sadly, this happens even in Christian relationships. Christian friendships aren't perfect. You and I aren't perfect. Why would we expect others in our groups to be?

Maybe you're familiar with the theologian Dietrich Bonhoeffer, a German pastor–theologian–seminary professor who was executed by the Nazis just before the end of World War II. Bonhoeffer wrote a book entitled *Life Together*. In it he discusses why so many relationships among and between Christians fall apart in groups. He says it is because of the "wish-dream." We have a wish, a dream, that our relationships, our Christian friendships will all be perfect. Yet, in a group, in a friendship, it is easy enough to withdraw, and that is what people do. We object to one person in the group, or one event, or one characteristic, and we say to ourselves that it is too much. Withdrawing ourselves breaks the fellowship, the Christian bond. Our thoughts usually go something like this: I wish this person wasn't always late; I wish he/she didn't talk so much; I wish he/she wouldn't give so much advice; I wish he/she wasn't so negative; I wish he/she didn't interrupt me so much, etc., etc., etc. These are wish-dreams, and the only place a wish-dream gets us is further and further out of Christian friendship, and further and further from Christ.

On and on we can go, eliminating all sorts of possible Christian relationships and groups from our lives, because they are not perfect. The wish-dream is a destroyer. Living like Christians means loving our neighbor as ourselves. It means exercising forgiveness. The truth of this is that we have to rely on the power of the Holy Spirit to do it. The truth of this is that it is hard, and frankly, too few have the stomach for it.

Nevertheless, the fact is that these imperfect experiences of friendship are what we have in this world. They are an appetizer for the beautiful and fulfilled friendships of heaven. Will we see those old friends who have been a bulwark in our lives and embrace them again? Yes, if we all have kept the faith. Will we see those Christian friends who have hurt us and dismissed us as unworthy? Yes, if we have kept the faith. At that reunion in eternity, I can foresee that we will embrace, perhaps weep together, forgive one another, and be restored in relationship again. The truth of the Scripture always stands: in Christ, all things are held together (Col 1:17).

There is an ancient allegory known as the Allegory of the Long Spoons that compares heaven and hell. It is attributed to Lithuanian Rabbi Haim. It is the story of a banquet hall. There are multitudes of tables, beautifully appointed, candelabras with gleaming candle light, flowers with the aroma of heaven, and the tables piled high with delicious foods of all sorts. At all of the tables were dinner guests who were seated across from each other and ravenously hungry. There was only one thing that was unusual. Each of the dinner guests had a long spoon of about three feet and a long fork of about three feet attached to their hands. The utensils were long enough to easily reach the food displayed in the center of the table, but the utensils were too long for any individual to be able to feed him or herself. Of course, this was frustrating. In the picture of hell, there was great crying and screaming and accusing and despair being expressed. The beautiful dining hall was filled with a cacophony of the horrible sounds of human selfishness. Death was imminent.

Nevertheless, the picture of heaven was entirely different. True, there was the same dining hall, similarly appointed, with the dining guests seated across from one another and the attached forks and spoons. Food was heaped in platters upon all the tables where they were seated. Yet, this scene was serene and joyful. There was laughter. There was an atmosphere of help and hope. What made the difference? In heaven, the dinner guests were using their long utensils to feed the people across the table from them.

Everyone was enjoying the food and the fellowship. Truly, table fellowship in heaven was table friendship. Everyone was sharing life and hope.

The Christian life of relationships can be pictured like this. No. It's not perfect. Not this side of heaven, but it is wonderful—once we learn how to share life together.

John Paul Sartre wrote a play entitled *No Exit*. In that play he portrays a scene where several people are in a waiting room. They are waiting for their entrance into heaven or hell. While they are in the waiting room, they begin to disparage one another, dislike one another, become irritated and hostile to one another. It is a terrible, miserable situation from which, it seems, there is no exit. It is Sartre's version of hell—being stuck together in life with other people. It is the very antithesis of the Christian life of spiritual friendship in which we are each called to love and cherish one another.

The third group that I want to mention is a group of Presbyterian clergy that was formed thirty-seven years ago at this writing. It began because four of us decided to try to bring a group together that would be all faithful Christian ministers, all in the same generational set, all Presbyterians, and all wanting to see the denomination renewed. My husband and I were invited to be part of this endeavor. We all tended to be mostly from a couple of key seminaries, Fuller in California, Gordon-Conwell in Massachusetts, and Princeton. We came together committed to meeting once a year for three to four days for the rest of our lives and being lifelong friends. We decided we would rotate leadership and locations in the country to meet. We would share the total expense equally. When we met, we would take time to each talk about our personal lives, share our prayer concerns, worship twice a day with music and prayer and Scripture, and have free afternoons to build our friendships together, or rest, or work on our Sunday sermons. We began with forty clergy, and today we are usually around thirty in a meeting. Without doubt, it has been one of the most important Christian groups in my life—and I think that is true for almost everyone in the group. It started because of the vision of four who reached out in friendship. It continued because of our friendships in Christ. I think many of us joined as young clergy in order to network. As time went on, we continued because it was a key place to belong and the tenderness of the relationships deepened. Now that several of us have retired, it has become even more precious to meet with old friends.

This past June, at this writing, one of our members died peacefully in his bed. He was one who was also in that small group in my twenties that

I wrote about earlier. Many of us gathered for his memorial service and to support his wife and family. The service was attended by at least five hundred people. People who had been in his circle of ministry, kids who had grown up in his youth ministry, adults who had been inspired by his facing a chronic disease and carrying on in faith, his children and grandchildren who celebrated his love for them demonstrated in a thousand ways over the years. The beauty of his Christian life was that he was "with" you in relationship, and he was stalwart in faith. He and his wife were my husband's and my closest friends. As it turned out, I preached his service, at his request. The text he chose was simple: "For me to live is Christ, and to die is gain" (Phil 1:21).

That is how it is in Christian friendship. Living in relationship with one another and seeking Christ in one another. Is that clergy group perfect? Of course not. Are friendships ever perfect in this life? No, of course not. Yet, they are a foretaste of the friendships we will all complete in eternity. The great reunion is ahead for us. A reunion of joy and fulfillment and the realization of relationships made for heaven. Christian spiritual friendships are eternal. They never end.

7

Friendship and Family

WHAT IF I WERE to say that you are your pretty-good family's best trajectory into the future, made in love and propelled in hope? And perhaps, just perhaps, you may find one of your closest lifelong friends in your own pretty-good family?

If you were born into a loving, pretty-good family, notice I didn't say "perfect" family, if you were born into a pretty-good family where you were welcomed and loved and your life was celebrated, well, you could believe that. You could embrace that. And maybe, just maybe, you had a sibling with a similar experience. Maybe your mother and father had prayed for you before you were born, and your sibling(s) did too! Your mother took every health precaution to be sure you would be born safe and well. Your parents decorated your nursery, and it was charming. When you were brought home, your parents were thrilled with you. They sent out announcements of your birth. Your older sibling(s) loved playing mama's helper with you. Your grandparents came in your first weeks of life to meet you and to acknowledge with your parents that you indeed were a wonderful representation of them all. Pictures were taken of you in the arms of the grandmas and grandpas and aunties and uncles. Baby gifts arrived for you from many of your family's friends. You were taken to the pediatrician. Your parents followed the doctor's prescription for how you should sleep and eat and be cared for in every detail. You were taken to church in your first year to be baptized or dedicated. You were surrounded with smiles and kisses and cuddles at every turn. Would you ever doubt that you were made in love and propelled in hope and your big sister or brother was a wonderful companion?

Perhaps when you were older, you would realize that you had been born into an extraordinarily loving family, not perfect, but a pretty-good family nonetheless. Your sibling(s) did too. My guess is that you would realize that not every child had the experience you did. Not every child is born into the world with the sure certainty that they were made in love and propelled in hope, and welcomed by any sibling(s) they may have. In fact, many, perhaps most in the world's population, could not identify with this statement.

They would say, the truth is that every child conceived is not conceived in love. Some children are conceived in violence. Some in desperation. Some are not even wanted. Some, perhaps many, children are born to parents too young, too immature, too irresponsible, too caught in disasters that overtake their own lives, too personally desperate to care much for their child—even if they wanted to. Some children conceived are aborted. Some children conceived are born into the world addicted to cocaine or with fetal alcohol syndrome. Some children born into this life are horribly abused and neglected. Some are born only to quickly die. Sadly, some children are turned out into the streets, to beg or prostitute, and children starve not for lack of love but for lack of food. Ironically, some children conceived are fed and housed and schooled and yet essentially overlooked by parents whose lives are "too busy," they would maintain. Some children are ignored, put down, or even terrorized by their siblings. All of these scenarios, these realities, are true. No one in these circumstances would affirm that they were made in love and propelled in hope and that their siblings were wonderful companions. Rather, life in the family for them could be characterized as an ever-occurring experience of fear and deprivation and even nightmare.

It has to be admitted. The world is a dangerous place. Sadly, the family can be no less so. How can anyone say that a child conceived is the family's best trajectory into the future, made in love and propelled in hope, surrounded by loving siblings? That's preposterous. It's naïve at best. It could be characterized as ignorant beyond description. True.

And yet . . . it was what God intended at creation, in Eden, before sin came slithering into human reality. God in creation was about giving us one another and in giving us one another, in that paradise, giving humanity the amazing power to create our own offspring, offspring that were to be their best trajectory into unfolding life, made in love and propelled in hope. Every human being who ever existed was created through some expression of the procreative act that was, from the beginning at origin, designed as an act of meaningful love. The root of the world is love. The original root of the family is love. The root of friendship is love.

Still, you may say, even if that kind of love is what God intended, that is not the world we live in. We live in a fallen world, and families are part of that. To such I would say, true. Look around at the current statistics on just our American families, not to even include the families of the world's population. So many are struggling, broken, suffering. So many children lack fathers. So many parents are working two or three jobs just to provide shelter and food. So many children are adrift in our society. So many families have members who are suffering with addictions.

The biblical description of the families of the Bible doesn't improve things. Right in the beginning, there is one brother killing another (Gen 4:8), and it doesn't get better. Remember Joseph's brothers who sold him into slavery (Gen 37:12–36). The fact is that the creation needs to be fully redeemed as it says in Rom 8. Included in that needed redemption are families. Followers of Christ who are called to live in love and care for one another have an opportunity to try to demonstrate what that sort of love and care look like. That's the mandate. The truth is, it isn't easy. The world is broken and so are its people—even the pretty-good ones.

So, let's start with a basic fact. There are no perfect families. It's pretty easy to understand why there are no perfect families. It's because there are no perfect people. You are not perfect, and neither am I. You may have been loved and doted on growing up, or perhaps you were turned out the door as soon as you could be on your own. In regards to this truth, it doesn't matter. There are no perfect families.

How could there be? Your parents were raised by their parents, and their parents by theirs, and on and on delving back into family history. In the midst of all the events that can occur in life that affect the lives of those who have come before us, there are ramifications that run down through the family tree. It's called multigenerational transmission. For example: my mother's father, a young foot soldier in World War I, was drafted and deployed to France. There on the battlefield of France trying to hold back the advancing enemy armies, he was one of the young men who was gassed. My generation read about it in the history books, but as I grew older I realized that that was my grandfather. I had never put that together before. Not surprisingly, my grandfather's experience had serious consequences for my mother, the oldest of his four children. He became an alcoholic and could never hold down a job for long after that. As you can imagine, it was difficult to have a stable childhood under that sort of circumstance. When my mother married my father, a good man and a good provider, and we children were born, we had a comfortable and secure growing up.

Yet once my mother said to me, "You know, Pam, you can always be proud to bring your friends home here."

I heard her and I thought, "Well, of course."

Years later I remembered her comment. It reflected the multigenerational transmission of her suffering as a child feeling less than secure in what I imagine were their frequently changing living circumstances. She wanted me to understand that I was blessed. Of course I was, but I was young, and I missed it. I missed what it meant to her.

When you think of your own family and you mentally travel back the generations and learn enough about their circumstances, you can see the strengths—yes; but also the sufferings, the cracks, or perhaps just the residue of those past generational experiences transmitting in some ways into your own life. Living in a warped or broken world, it makes sense that there are no perfect families.

Yet, because of Christ's redeeming work, there are some pretty-good families, and with intentional prayer and care, some of those families produce some pretty-good people. Among those pretty-good people, some pretty-good friendships can develop.

That is what I am writing about in this chapter. Friendship and families.

When we think about friendship and family, many of us feel uneasy. What does family have to do with friendship, we ask ourselves. Friendship is a relationship in an entirely different category. That's right. It is. Still, sometimes these two different types of relationship coincide, overlap, develop into a wonderful companionship that in time, sometimes, results in real friendship.

If you think as Aelred of Rievaulx did that friendship was a relationship of love between two people and Christ, a three-way relationship, there is no prohibition against finding that in one's own family, with a sibling, with a cousin, with a parent, or even an in-law. Of course, it can be complicated. These relationships, if developed into friendships, become what is known as "dual relationships." Dual relationships take skill to navigate successfully. For example, when a mother and a daughter or a father and son are real friends there are certain boundaries that must be respected. There are distinctive attitudes of love, respect, and honor. These boundaries exist because the relationship is cross-generational. There must be some personal distance, some willingness to tolerate with respect different opinions, some appreciation expressed of what each brings in love to enrich the relationship. Nevertheless, that is not so different from friends who are not familial. As one loves a friend, one respects certain aspects of that friend's life as too intimate, even for most friendships.

For example, occasionally, a mentor becomes a friend. When that happens, the mentor still retains in the history of the relationship that original mentor position, even though that would generally not be invoked by the mentor in a maturing friendship of equality. Nevertheless, from time to time, that old relationship will surface with a legitimate need of request for the mentor's wisdom. In that case if the mentor genuinely desires the friendship, he or she is wise to share what is requested but without assuming the distance of authority that was once a key part of that former relationship.

There are lots of people who minimize the value of their family of origin, as well as thinking that their life in their particular family was simply an accident of nature. They say to themselves, "I just somehow landed in this family. Once I'm old enough, I'm free of these people. My friends are my family." If you think this is an exaggeration, think again. This is not an uncommon sentiment. From time to time I see posted on greeting cards or plaques or even bumper stickers the statement: "Family is what I was born into. Friends are the family I choose." To this I would say, well, yes and no.

The truth is that you are the product genetically and psychologically of your family. There is the fact that in multiple physiological and psychological ways you will never be entirely free of them. To a certain extent, you are them. Or better put perhaps, you are their best trajectory into the future—whether they intended that or not. It just is.

No one can deny that there are some terribly destructive families, dangerous even. The very best thing that anyone can do who comes out of that fulcrum of dysfunction and possibly even evil is to get clear and stay clear. I once had a student who told me that her parents had been serial killers. If that was true, it's not hard to understand why she moved far away and wasn't in touch. Surely, that is the dark side of human existence, but what about the bright side, the fairly healthy, emotionally and spiritually, pretty-good family? Let's think about what is possible in those pretty-good family relationships.

There's a pretty-good family described in the New Testament. They were siblings who were close friends of Jesus. Lazarus, Mary, and Martha lived in Bethany, a bit east outside of Jerusalem where Jesus would frequently stop to visit, to share a meal, to take off his sandals and rest a while. You know places like that in your life, places where you can visit and "crash," to put it in contemporary slang. There's an account in the New Testament of Jesus visiting these dear friends bringing with him his twelve disciples. It might have gone something like this:

Jesus arriving at the house and calling out: Hey, Lazarus, Mary, Martha, are you here? Pause. Oh good. We were heading for Jerusalem and getting near, when we thought we'd just drop in for a visit on our way. I don't want to miss you when I'm this close. Pause. This may not be convenient, I know. It's almost dinnertime. Pause. Do we want to stay for dinner? Oh, that sounds great. I've got the other twelve with me, you know. Pause. Wonderful to be here with you!

Now imagine, if you will, how it would be for you, if thirteen grown men arrived unannounced at your house for an impromptu dinner. Never mind that you considered them dear to you. Never mind if they took off their shoes or not. That would be the least of your concerns at that point. Thirteen grown men. Thirteen grown and hungry men. That's a lot of food and a lot of cooking and a lot of dishes. And remember, there was no take-out in those days, and men evidently didn't help in the kitchen. No matter how you look at it, Martha and Mary were scrambling. Well, anyway, as it turns out, Martha was scrambling. Mary seemed to be irresistibly drawn to Jesus's every word. She spent her time with Jesus. At first that was good, Martha thought. Mary was welcoming them and making them feel at home, but then, after a while, Martha checked the living room, and there was her sister, looking serenely relaxed, sitting at Jesus's feet and drinking in his every word. Martha had fish on the fire, vegetables to chop, rice to cook, bread baking. "I just can't take this anymore," Martha must have muttered something like that to herself and burst into the room to appeal to Jesus to tell her sister to get into the kitchen and start helping her. However, Jesus uses it as an object lesson, albeit to the distress of Martha, by telling Martha that Mary was doing what was the very most important thing, learning and listening and trusting in him. Martha must have been nonplussed!

Now, do you think Martha was filled with sisterly love and admiration for her sister, Mary, at that point? Do you think that Martha thought, "Oh, my dear spiritual sister, Mary, she is not only my sister but my dearest friend in life." I doubt it. I can imagine they probably had a squabble, a rather big squabble in fact. Right in front of their company! Now this happened between two of Jesus's very closest friends in life whom he loved dearly. This happened in a pretty-good family, not perfect, but pretty-good. The reality is that things like misunderstandings and squabbles happen in families—just like they do between friends who are not family. The question always is, how is it resolved? Did forgiveness take place? And, of course, what happened after that? We know from the biblical accounts that Mary and Martha and Lazarus continued to be some of Jesus's closest friends. In fact, he stayed with them the night before he rode into Jerusalem to face his crucifixion. Perhaps Mary was there at the foot of the cross.

There's an interesting couple prominently named in the New Testament, two Jewish converts to Christ, Priscilla and Aquila, who are expelled from Rome for being of Jewish descent and who meet Paul in Corinth—presumably because they were all tentmakers for a living. These two turned out to be powerful leaders and close friends of Paul who entrusted them with the Corinthian church as he continued on in his missionary evangelistic travels. At one point, the text tells us that Priscilla even instructs Apollos (Acts 18:26), one of the emerging church's primo preachers, because he was ignorant of the baptism Jesus commanded and was instead preaching the repentance baptism of John. Culturally, for Priscilla, a woman, to instruct Apollos, a male leader, is extraordinarily unusual. It is also striking that it is reported in the text. It is an important testimony to Priscilla's ministry and influence. Priscilla and Aquila worked together as a strong team for decades and were foundational for the early church. Paul calls them co-workers and partners in the gospel. They were husband and wife. Were they friends? One assumes so. Certainly, I think we can assume that there were at the very least significant aspects of friendship in their relationship. They were committed to one another, as pretty-good married couples generally are, and they both loved Christ and served the church. If Aelred's definition of friendship applies as two people who love one another and Christ, one can safely assume that they are a New Testament example of a husband and wife who were friends.

Friendships within families and between family members are possible—so long as we concede that just as there are no perfect families, and no perfect people, there are no perfect friends—inside or outside the family. Once we accept that fact, we find that the great doors of friendship possibilities swing open, and we are afforded an abundance of life-giving joy and companionship. Some of it right in the backyard of our own families!

It's always fun and interesting to travel back in the history of world thought to explore how friendship in the family was understood by some of the great minds. For example, Aristotle believed that a husband and wife were an example of friendship, albeit an unequal one because, true to his culture, the husband, the male, was superior to the woman, the female. However, in this respect, Aristotle who maintained that friendships, real friendships, "good" relationships, were possible only between men of virtue, seems to have classified marital friendship as also among the "good" relationships. Noted it was of lesser good than a male friendship, because it was with a woman, but Aristotle, interestingly enough, did not discount the importance of the husband-and-wife friendship.

In church history we discover expressions of the reality of friendship between and among family members. Ambrose, the bishop of Milan from AD 374 to 397, who had previously been a provincial governor, is a good place to start. The very center of Western Christianity at that time was Milan. We could think of it as the Rome of its day. You may remember this story. Augustine, of North Africa, who became one of the greatest of the church fathers, was at that time a young man of talent and intellect, an orator, not a Christian, come to Milan to gain fame and fortune as a professor of rhetoric. There he heard the bishop preach, and one day in the garden heard a child's voice say: "Take up and read." He took a New Testament, read Paul's Letter to the Romans, and was converted. Ambrose was the most significant influence on young Augustine in his early development as a Christian leader. Augustine was profoundly affected by Ambrose and his teaching. Later when Augustine himself had achieved prominence as a Christian leader, he wrote about friendship. This is what he wrote:

> Now (in friendship) we have agreement in things human and divine, with benevolence and love, in Christ Jesus our Lord, our most true peace.[1]

He had been influenced by Ambrose's writing as bishop to his clergy. It is one of the most significant writings in Christian history, *On the Duties of the Clergy*, a three-volume work for priests and other clerics whom

1. Carmichael, *Friendship*, 58.

Ambrose was training in Milan. Entitled *De officiis*, and composed between AD 386 and 391, it was the first sustained treatise on Christian ethics and pastoral theology,[2] and it emphasizes the importance of friendship.

> Open your heart to your friend so that he will be faithful to you, and so that you will know joy in your own life from him: for "a faithful friend is the medicine of life, the grace of immortality" (Sir. 6:16; III.129).[3]

Here "Ambrose exhorts his clergy to be friends to one another," maintaining that "friendship is integral to the lifestyle of a Christian minister."[4]

It's important to note that it was Ambrose who was the first to collect together, in one place, the obvious biblical material on friendship. Nevertheless, as he did that, he did not neglect Cicero, who wrote: "For friendship is nothing else than an accord in all things, human and divine, conjoined with mutual goodwill and affection."[5]

Ambrose's writings, along with Cicero's, were important to Aelred of Rievaulx in the 1100s when Aelred was writing on spiritual friendship. Aelred noted that for Ambrose the hallmark of Christian friendship was intimate godly sharing. Ambrose took to heart Jesus's sharing with his disciples: "You are my friends if you do what I command you. . . . I have called you friends, because I have made known to you everything that I have heard from my father" (John 15:15).

Ambrose maintained that Jesus "has given us the pattern of friendship we should follow"; to do the will of our friend, open whatever secrets we have in our hearts, and know what is in theirs.[6] A friend hides nothing then; if he is true, he pours out his heart, as the Lord Jesus poured out the mysteries of the Father. This challengingly intimate sharing, implying a search for oneness yet potentially more open and dynamic than Cicero's already-established mutual agreement, was becoming the central definition of Christian friendship.

Yet, Ambrose's closest friends, it seems, were not his clergy colleagues, but his elder sister, Marcellina, and his brother, Satyrus. Marcellina, a woman of great faith, took vows as a dedicated Christian virgin and a

2. Carmichael, *Friendship*, 51.
3. Carmichael, *Friendship*, 47.
4. Carmichael, *Friendship*, 46.
5. Carmichael, *Friendship*, 26.
6. Ambrose, as quoted in Carmichael, *Friendship*, 50

female Christian leader. She was an important close confidant of Ambrose. Satyrus left his own career and came to Milan to assist Ambrose with his administrative ministry. These three siblings, much like Lazarus, Martha, and Mary, were the closest of friends.

If one continues to dig into past history of Christian leaders who were not only relatives but friends, we would very soon come across two men who were known as the Cappadocian fathers. They were two of the most important theologians of the early church in the fourth century, Basil of Caesarea and his brother, Gregory of Nyssa.

They were trained classically and so they were steeped in the friendship tradition. It is important to note that the classical tradition had been influenced by Philo of Alexandria writing in the first half of the first century. Philo shifted the ground of true friendship from human virtue (Aristotle) to shared faith in God. This changed the whole perception of friendship in the Christian world.

Carmichael writes: "It now becomes axiomatic that friendship between Christians is grounded in common commitment to Christ, a paradigm shift that widened the community of friendship from the select few (as it had been to the ancients) to the entire committed Church, including women."[7]

This evolution of the concept of friendship is a fascinating account—even in this brief highlight of its developments. Now it is that "the true friendship that is the perfection of Christian love springs from faith and involves forgiveness and renewal. Ambrose expects it to be common, uniting not just the few but all whom caritas 'love' embrace together. In principle and in potential, the loving goodwill and forgiveness that extends to all should draw all humanity into this new community of friendship."[8]

This moves us from understanding friendship classically as possible to only a few good, virtuous men, to the possibility of true friendship for those who love Christ (including women) and are committed to one another.[9]

But the question has to be asked: Why attribute a whole chapter of this book to friendship and families? Surely this topic could have been handled deftly in another chapter as a brief aside.

7. Carmichael, *Friendship*, 41.

8. Carmichael, *Friendship*, 51.

9. In this chapter, I was greatly helped and taught by Liz Carmichael, an Oxford scholar, in her thoroughly researched and documented book, *Friendship: Interpreting Christian Love*. I would recommend it to anyone who is looking for a detailed and excellent summary of the topic.

The answer is motivated by my own pastoral concern for the rather alarming statistics of eroding mental health in our society today. Increasingly, studies are reporting that the greatest psychological issue reported in the United States is loneliness. Our society's focus on individualism and independence as the highest of all personal goods has resulted in the greatest number of single households ever reported in US history—and I should add that is with the actual increase of young college grads living at home in their parents' basements. While reported divorces are declining, the incidents of divorces in our society in the past fifty years has been a wrecking ball on generations who have grown up not trusting, not believing that good marriages are possible, not seeing marriage as an avenue of building a life of worth and stability in their world.

As a clergyperson, I can tell you that it is the minority of couples who come seeking to be married in the church who are not already living together. This is a huge change from fifty years ago. Even though all the statistics on living together before marriage seem to demonstrate that "trying it out," that is, living together, to see if a marriage will work, actually turns out to be detrimental to the projected longevity of the marriage, the trend persists. The reasoning is that a trial run is a hedge against failure. However, what often happens is that after a few years, when life has become normalized as a couple, one or the other may decide, seemingly suddenly, to get out, leaving the remaining partner feeling desperate and used up. Often this leaves children, born to unmarried couples, floundering. It is a whole lonely scene of brokenhearted people trying to revive their lives and feeling, sometimes desperately feeling, lonely.

My question is: What could help? It's not the only solution, but it is one approach to encourage people to take another look at their own families, to consider if, given the vast amount of life experience they share, or the loved ones they share if they are in-laws, that there, right before their eyes, could be a wonderful and supportive brother or sister, or cousin, or father or mother or mother-in-law. Not every friend has to be the same age. One who is already cognizant of you and your life and predisposed in many cases to sharing life with you more than you may have previously thought may be the perfect cherished new friend in your life. And there they are, right before your nose!

Think about your brother, younger or older, or your once-irritating sister who growing up was always wearing your clothes. Could it be that there is a future, valuable friend? What if you began to phone regularly or invite him or her to meet you for dinner? What if you could get past the old stereotypes and get to know one another as adults? You might find a growing relationship of friendship that becomes more and more meaningful.

Sometimes it just happens, a realization, even a joke, and the relationship shifts towards friendship. My younger brother (he would say, much younger) somehow got the idea that I was the smart one of the two of us. "Oh, no," I would say to him, when he half-jokingly referred to it. Then, something happened that was fortuitous. He came across a box in the basement that belonged to our mother and contained my old report cards. Now, lest I create the wrong impression, my grades were good, but they were definitely not all A's. Nevertheless, guess whose grades were all A's in school? I think you know: my super brainy little brother.

Now, do I have to say that this comes up with some frequency in our conversations? He says, "Boy, those report cards, Sis." And he chuckles. "What were you doing?" he asks me.

"Well, you know," I always reply, "Spending time with friends!"

Why do I go into such a silly story discussing the formation of family friendships? Because it's as good a story as any to illustrate that most everything that can be part of shared life experience with siblings has the potential to begin to spark a different kind of relationship—a friendship that could mean the difference between an enriching companionship and loneliness.

In addition, I hope this will encourage the married to seek to initiate, build, or enhance friendship with their spouse. The greatest satisfaction in marriage is reported by those who call their spouse their best friend. This is reported in studies of both men and women.[10] "Well, that is never going to work in our case," you may say, and maybe you're right. Not all marriages are friendships. However, if one were interested in promoting friendship with one's spouse it could bring a wealth of additional joy to life. Some wonder how that could ever happen. The answer is that it would happen in much the same manner as one builds a friendship with anyone, with the added benefit of sexual intimacy. Daily or regularly initiating loving or appreciative words or compliments, courtesy, and invitations to join together in activities that the other enjoys. These are many of the same ways that friendships are built with anyone. In my pastoral counseling practice I have encouraged parishioners or clients to work at complimenting their spouse at least once a day,

10. Take a look at Gottman and Silver, *Seven Principles.*

something sincere and true. It's not surprising that within a month or so, the marriage warms up and more is shared in friendship.

Friendships are the treasure of life's relationships, and there are no off-limits in regards to them. It is through friendships that one not only finds deepening joy but a deepening understanding of oneself, a stretching, a growing of the soul as one reaches out in love and learns to abide in love.

And speaking of reaching out, let us remember that it doesn't just have to be meeting some brand-new person at the book club or the sports club. A new and valuable friend may be as close as your own family. That's not just pretty-good but very-good news!

8

Friendship and Lament

LAMENT: THE EXPRESSION OF the heart's weeping over great loss.

It was just last June that I sat with my two closest friends, a married couple, friends of my entire adult lifetime. My husband had traveled home to preach. We three were on the patio of their place in Pasadena, California. Just the three of us, but crowded with the memories of life shared and friendship cherished, over forty-plus years. First joining together in friendship in a small group of Bible study and prayer, we connected deeply early on, worshipping together, vacationing together. When my first husband died, they were a rock for me. The next year after, I moved to the Pasadena area, and we rented a house together. Our kids played together like cousins. Together, we went to seminary, a graduate school for those preparing for ministry. It was they who introduced me to my now-husband, John. We shared our lives together. We shared the Lord together.

Now, my friend Don was in his wheelchair, his regular seat and mode of transport these past few years. His wife, Karen, was, as ever, the one who had cared for him for decades, loved him loyally. She faced down into near oblivion her deep disappointment at his condition and her personal inner struggle with it. She worked hard to protect him from any more suffering and disappointment at the obvious progression of the disease and to protect him from impulsivity and impatience, signs of the mental effects of disease. Born into strength and vitality, knowing himself as that person, he had been cut down and had grown increasingly impatient with his limitations.

As a Christian minister, he continued to pastor people with his caring, his voice, his counsel, his prayers, his faith. He kept strong in his faith, never wavering. They were together in the faith journey, as always. For years now, Parkinson's disease was his companion, her companion, and therefore my companion as well.

There had been those times of carefree exuberance in our twenties and some of our thirties before he was diagnosed. Now, he was stolid, stalwart. Keeping on keeping on. What started out for us as a robust relationship, full of youthful, shared faith and laughter and exuberance—adventurous, resilient, like an unsinkable inner tube in the laughing river rapids—had metamorphosed over the decades. It was no longer a lightly floating inner tube. It had entirely changed. Now our relationship had been fired and refined like fine porcelain, cherished, translucent with light. Like fine porcelain, we handled it carefully, tenderly. We all knew—something could break at any moment.

So that day last June, we sat. The three of us on the Pasadena patio, quietly, peacefully, being alone together, and crowded, as I said, only with memories.

She said: "I love this time of the evening." The twilight.

He nodded, yes.

"I do too," I said. "Look, even as the darkness falls we can still see the outline of the tree branches. Even in the dark, we can still see light."

We were all quiet, musing. Then, she stood up, gently, so as not to dissipate the moment. "Better get you back for bed at the health center," she said to him. The health center was just across the way from her apartment.

I stood up and bent down to kiss his head. "Good night," I said softly.

"I love you, Pameo," he said.

"I love you too," I said tenderly.

The next morning, we were awakened by an urgent pounding on the apartment door by a messenger from the health center. "Come quickly. Come! Come now!" was the breathless message. We went.

There he was in his bed. His face, so often contorted with pain, was serene, calm, at peace. I thought to myself, he fell asleep and awoke in heaven. After all these years of suffering, he had the peaceful passing of the beloved.

He had chosen for his memorial service the verse "For me to live is Christ and to die is gain" (Phil 1:21). That was really, truly, rock-solid, spot-on who he was. He'd suffered in the living and now was in the midst of the Great Gain. Hundreds came to his farewell service. I'm not exaggerating.

People flew in for it. People spoke of how his faith in the midst of decades of suffering had impacted their lives. Some who had been youth in his ministry years ago testified as adults that he had changed their lives for the better. My husband and I both spoke. His wife and loyal children each spoke, lifting him up with much deserved honor. I hope he knew. I believe he knew. A life well lived had its final earthly tribute offered up with profound love.

Then, after a few days, the quietness, the absence, the aloneness, the gone-ness. He had been lifted into glory, as they say. We still walked the hard ground of this life. Now, I was feeling it, really feeling it, grieving, uttering the lament for a friend.

We seldom talk about lament in our culture, our lives today. It seems an old term, restricted to the Old Testament, mainly present in the book of Psalms. It is the weeping of the soul, the parting, the anguish, the yearning. A lament in grief would be something like this: "Now, O Lord, you who have come to our beloved one, come to us, into our very souls; fill those aching spaces with your love and grace, for we are lamenting our loss. Now, to you, the God of all comfort [as Paul writes in 2 Cor 1:3–5], we pray. Comfort us."

We see a good example of lament in the Old Testament with King David and his much-loved son Absalom. Absalom betrayed his father. He rebelled against his father king and tried to seize the crown with armed conflict. The result is that Absalom was killed in battle. He was killed—even though David explicitly gave his generals instructions going into battle not to harm Absalom. When David received the news of Absalom's death, he cried out in lament: "Oh Absalom, Absalom, my son, would that I had died instead of you" (2 Sam 18:33). Such is a father's heart-wrenching grief. I doubt that any loving parent would disbelieve David's feelings at that time. It was an authentic example of a pure lament ripped from the heart.

It would be difficult to expect that any one of us is exempt from the possibility of betrayal when Jesus, our Lord, himself, experienced such a murderous betrayal by a very close friend. Judas Iscariot was one of his chosen disciples, one of the twelve. Judas, whose motivations cannot be clearly ascertained from Scripture, sought out the company of the high priest and his counselors to offer to betray Jesus. Perhaps Judas hoped that if Jesus were threatened with arrest and trial, he would summon all his power and proceed to become the king of Israel, casting out the Romans and bringing Israel into a kingdom of power. Perhaps Judas, dismayed by Jesus's acceptance of a very expensive nard for his body, followed by Jesus's rebuff of Judas's protest (John 12:1–8), came to a breaking point in his faith and commitment. At any rate, for his betrayal of Jesus, the temple authorities paid Judas thirty pieces of silver. We know of the events from the Gospel records. What will you pay me to betray Jesus to you, he asks (Matt 26:15). And so Judas betrayed Jesus with a kiss (Matt 26:47–50) in the garden of Gethsemane.

It even seems that Peter may be a betrayer when he warms himself before the high priest's courtyard fire and is asked by a maid if he is with Jesus. Peter's reply, "I do not know the man" (Matt 26:52), is a betrayal as well. Yet while Peter's denial was a result of imminent danger and reasonable fear and later repented of, Judas's betrayal was premeditated, unrepentant, and unredeemed. We know how these events play out for Judas and Peter. Peter, repentant with hot tears, an authentic lament, and subsequently forgiven, becomes a great champion of the faith, of the church. Judas hangs himself (Matt 27:5). Judas becomes the very embodiment of what it means to betray.

When we think deeply about human friendship, its joys and its blessings, we have to acknowledge that there in the company of joy can be sorrow. The fragility of life intrudes.

We know it in the face of death, but there is also the malleability of human relationship in the midst of the complicated inner factors of each individual. There is the ever-present power of the broken world intruding on our character and on our very souls. Sin lurks, bringing jealousy, anger, selfishness, ambition, unacknowledged motivations, destruction. All persons do not live "wholeheartedly." They do not live transparently, genuinely open, even with their friends. The truth is that while many friends may be gained in a lifetime, and sometimes in one blessed season of life, some will be lost—and not just through benign neglect. There are those lost through death, of course, and sadly, it must be said, some are lost through betrayal. While some friendships will last us into eternity, some will need to be redeemed in eternity, and hopefully are. It is the loss in this earthly life that is the particularly hard fact. Knowing this, experiencing this personally, there is the lament.

When we look at the letters of Paul, we hear the plaintive strain of a lament when Paul mentions a former close companion, a co-worker and disciple who left him. Paul writes from his imprisonment in Rome: "Demas, in love with this present world, has deserted me" (2 Tim 4:9). That Demas was, for a while, a part of Paul's inner circle seems to be additionally verified by Paul's writing in Colossians. Paul, writing to Colossae, sends this final greeting. "Luke, the beloved physician, and Demas greet you" (Col 4:14). In all probability, Demas's departure was experienced by Paul as a betrayal. Later, as Paul speaks to Demas's desertion, he adds a lonely lament: "Only Luke is with me" (2 Tim 4:11).

Throughout history there is this ongoing story of betrayal in relationship. Most are familiar with the line from Shakespeare's play *Julius Caesar*. Caesar, having become emperor of Rome, once a great republic, accumulated numerous enemies among the Roman senate. Finally, in an assassination plot executed in the senate house, Caesar is stabbed multiple times by the members of the senate. The last one to stab him was his much loved protégé, Brutus. My guess is that we have all heard this question of realization of betrayal, Caesar's words to his beloved Brutus, *Et tu, Brute?* And you, Brutus? Here in just three words with a precious name uttered, one hears the incredulity and pain of betrayed love, anguish, and the deep lament of the dying heart.

These are among some of the most dramatic, public examples of betrayal. Everyday betrayals take place among and between the rest of us in ordinary life as well. I personally know of three women whose husbands divorced them and married their former wives' best friends. Clearly, a life crisis of huge proportions—the betrayal of both a husband and a best friend. Here the loud strain of lament fades in time, but still haunts the heart.

Even at a young age, the human heart can be fickle, still growing into its mature strength. Today, preteens and teens have bracelets and necklaces they share with for-that-moment best friend. BFF (best friends forever) is engraved upon them. These are regularly changed, disposed of, and abandoned. Admittedly in some cases, the loss is more than a simple removal of a bracelet. It is the lament of a young girl.

It seems clear that we human beings, while pretty good at making connections with others, and pretty good at sensing and understanding who is really a friend, are also pretty susceptible to being misled or simply not picking up the relational clues that would telegraph lack of full commitment to our relationship with another person. As it turns out, we tend to forget that human beings are also pretty good at deceiving others. Again, the truth of it.

Saying all this may seem to imply that seeking friendships isn't worth the risk, but that is not at all the case. If I believed that, I would never have written this book. When you think of the number of friendships you have made over the years, my guess is that you can count on one hand, or even a few fingers, the numbers of betrayals you have experienced, if any at all. My personal research seems to indicate that about 25 percent of people with good lifetime friendships have never experienced a betrayal.

I think of it this way; there are x number of bridges in the US that could possibly collapse because of the present condition of the infrastructure. We all know that. Still, when I am traveling, even around town, I don't intend to avoid bridges. Bridges lead me to where I want to be. It's the same with making friendships. Friendships are where we want to be if we want to live happy, satisfied, meaningful, joyful lives.

Annie Dillard, the Pulitzer Prize–winning author, writes in *Teaching a Stone to Talk* about this need that we all have to be in relationship with others. She writes about "our complex and inexplicable caring for each other and our life together here. This is given. It is not learned."[1] Dillard is right. Human beings are, at the core, community, relational creatures. It is almost as if we can't help ourselves not to reach out to others. Hardwired this way by our Creator, when it comes right down to it, we are no good at going it alone.

To emphasize the truthful observance from philosopher Martin Buber, "All real living is meeting,"[2] we agree that nothing in this life replaces the full, open, authentic, respectful, caring relationship with another human soul. Buber has it exactly. It is the very definition of what it means to live meaningfully as a human being.

So having dealt with the most difficult friendship-ending possibilities, death and some of the extreme betrayal examples, we are still faced with the reality that some friendships just end. Usually these friendships fall into a relationship category other than what we think of as real friendships. Mostly, these endings are not dramatic. They can be exceptionally quiet. They can be tiptoe endings. There is no big public awareness. They are the friendships, the relationships, the associations that just slip away— often before we even realize it or even notice it happening. In those cases, it seems that we are too occupied with other parts of our lives to lament.

In this category fall most of the come-and-go friendships and acquaintances that were mentioned in chapter 2. At their best, they are fine while they last. They include the great next-door neighbor who puts their house up for sale in order to move to another state. Oh, yes, we shake our

1. Dillard, as quoted by Rohr, *Falling Upward*, 53.
2. Buber, *I and Thou*, 11.

head and wish they weren't moving, but in most cases this is not a heart-break for us. They include the couple in church who were always a couple you thought it would be good to get to know. Somehow you never quite took the time to connect with them—at least not much more than over church coffee. Then, you find out that they changed churches. They include the retirement of the owner of the corner dry cleaner with whom you had established a pleasant, chatty relationship. They are people who are part of the fabric of our lives but not central to our personal happiness. It's not that they're not important as people. Of course, they are. It is rather that they haven't made their way into the inner circle of our heart's affection. They will go on their way happily—and we will do the same. Here, at these end-ings, no lament is uttered. In fact, a lament would seem artificial. It is not a rending of the heart.

In the whole range of loss of friendships, we have touched on the most painful and the least painful, but what of the intermediate sorts of losses that are not loss of life but the withdrawal of love? These also cause deep personal lament, for they too fall under the category of betrayal. Many of the classical philosophical and/or theological writers—Aristotle, Cicero, Augustine, Jerome, Aelred—as well as Scripture itself, all agree that there are some legitimate means for ending a friendship. Yet, if one has given oneself wholeheartedly to the friend, how can there ever be a means for ending a friendship, you may ask.

Aelred himself has struggled with that. He points out that friendship requires four elements: love and affection, security and happiness. These are altered when a friendship ends. Leaving the consideration of love to the last, let's think of what happens to affection when a friendship has ended. What does the dissolution look like of affection, that inner feeling that demonstrates outwardly? It may be the absence of warm welcome when one unexpectedly comes upon a former friend in a restaurant. Affection would smile. There is no such smile when affection has dissolved. To con-tinue with security, consider how it would be for you if you had an inkling that your personal confidences were being shared with others without your consent. Such is the uneasiness that causes the withdrawal of that confident feeling of absolute security in another's confidences. Certainly when affec-tion and security absent themselves, happiness, that inner joy, becomes sad-ness as the pleasure of sharing regular relationship in friendly conversation absents itself. Love, however, the most important part of Christian virtue should not be withdrawn. True, "conduct may require the withdrawal of friendship, but never of love," writes Aelred.[3]

This is true, even in the midst of the six reasons that Aelred lists as legitimate reasons for ending a friendship.[4]

To think that there are at least six legitimate reasons for ending a friendship—a friendship that has been cherished and tender, seems hard to believe. How could there be so many? How could any of the reasons Aelred lists even take place? Since some of Aelred's descriptions can be combined, let me summarize them as three.

The first is the betrayal of confidences.[5] One of the quickest ways to conclude a friendship is to eliminate the factor of absolute trust. One of my colleagues at the counseling center has wisely observed that to continue in relationship, people need safety and satisfaction in a relationship. Safety in confidences shared is an absolute foundation of friendship. Without the valuing of confidentiality on the part of both parties, the friendship quickly evaporates because of lack of trust.

However, below the surface of this requirement for confidentiality in relationship can lie complications. It seems that these complications manifest themselves depending on the degree of privacy a friend requires. For example, imagine that you are in a committed friendship with another person who has a higher standard for privacy (note that privacy is not the same thing as confidentiality) than you do. Imagine that your friend is away on a wonderful trip to Hawaii. Imagine that someone comments on the absence of your friend at some sort of gathering you attend and you comment: Yes, he/she is on a vacation in Hawaii. That satisfies the inquiring party and seems as if that is not a violation of confidentiality. However, this may be considered a very private matter to your friend, and may cause your friend to confuse confidentiality with privacy and act accordingly. It is important in friendship, when one has access to another's personal activities and plans, to inquire: Should I consider this confidential? This caution will often avoid a serious disruption or even the loss of a friendship.

Another aspect of this that may surprise some is the good news a friend receives and happily and initially shares only with you. As a friend, you experience this as good news as well. We all know how we experience getting good news. We want to share it! It's too good to keep quiet.

3. Aelred of Rievaulx, *Spiritual Friendship*, 103.

4. Aelred of Rievaulx, *Spiritual Friendship*, 96–103.

5. Aelred of Rievaulx, *Spiritual Friendship*, 97.

So here, a word of caution. Slow down! It's important to understand that it is not your news to share. It belongs to your friend, and if you share it first with others, your friend is robbed of the joyous experience of sharing with others and robbed of the first flush of excitement and congratulations that comes upon the inbreaking of good news. It is, in a sense, a violation of confidentiality—even though it is done with the best of intentions and fueled by your shared joy. Thus, disclosing confidences, even if it is meant innocently, can be destructive to a friendship and unintentionally cause loss and lament.

The second is slander and backbiting. There are those fickle friends who begin unaccountably to accuse the faithful friend of motives or actions or beliefs that are not in any way true. If this is done publicly, it can be believable to others. Here is someone who has been a friend to this person, they reason. Of course, the accuser knows what this person is really like.

When done publicly the intention is to harm not only the individual personally but their reputation. Aelred elaborates on this offense by writing: "Slander injures the reputation and extinguishes love."[6] Slander of this sort is almost impossible to undo.

Yet, why would someone called a friend engage in this sort of behavior knowing that it would surely end the friendship? What could have happened for this to take place? Multiple possibilities arise. Perhaps the offending friend has been told something damaging about their friend and, without examining its truth, simply believes it and then becomes an accuser. It is a difficult realization to understand that a significant number of people receive, without filter, any claim against another without any sort of legitimate verification. For them, if it is said or if it is printed, then it must be true. Advertisers, especially, have found this to be a very profitable characteristic of a portion of the human population. Another possibility is that there is some sort of benefit or profit socially or monetarily to the offending friend that may supersede in their mind their loyalty. And finally, perhaps it is simply that the friendship was not of such value to the betrayer. Realizing any of this causes one to lament.

There is an old story about a public slander that makes the point. A disgruntled man in a priest's parish slandered the priest. After a while, the offender, overcome by guilt, went to the priest to repent of his slander. The priest, relieved, accepted the apology but asked the penitent to climb with him up into the bell tower of the church. The priest carried with him a

---

6. Aelred of Rievaulx, *Spiritual Friendship*, 96.

pillow and a knife. Upon reaching the pinnacle of the bell tower, the priest turned to the offender and said to him, I accept your apology, but please note what I am about to do and what the result is that follows. At that point, the priest slit the pillow open and shook it out from atop the bell tower. Feathers were scattered everywhere. There were so many that eventually one could not even see where all the feathers had drifted. This is what happens when you slander another person. To a certain extent, the damage never ends, the sad priest explained.

Slander is a knife to the heart of reputation. The heart's blood that is lost can never be completely restored. There, only lament remains.

And finally, the third reason for ending a friendship is that it could harm a family member or a friend who also depends on your loyalty and support.[7] For example: a friend who is a friend to you but spreads rumors about your spouse; a friend who harms or abuses one of your children; a friend who, using your friendship as a credential, gains access to your relatives' accounts and cheats them. Whereas friendship is one of the highest relationships that one can attain, it can never be allowed to harm those of your family circle or those for whom their livelihood depends upon you. This sort of offence to a friend is a result of the vice of pride. For some unfathomable reason, the offending friend believes that their standing with you in friendship overrides your other family and personal relationships. It must not be tolerated, and maintaining the friendship in the light of this harmful conduct to others is not a demonstration of virtue, which friendship is meant to encourage and promote, but rather a demonstration of weakness and cowardliness, a lack of honor. The friendship must end, and deep lament occurs.

Here, I think of Jerome, who is quoted in Aelred: "A friendship that can end, was never true."[8]

All of this exploration of betrayal of friendship leads us to an important question that Peter asked Jesus: "How many times do I forgive a brother [a fellow believer]? Seven times?"

"Not seven times," Jesus responded, "but seventy times seven" (Matt 18:21–22).

In other words, forgiveness among the body of Christ should be offered readily when relationship restoration is sought and genuine repentance takes place (see Matt 18:15–17).

---

7. Aelred of Rievaulx, *Spiritual Friendship*, 102.

8. Aelred of Rievaulx, *Spiritual Friendship*, 59.

Of course, wounding has taken place and some caution in the restored relationship is merited, but coming to forgiveness and embrace is the finest expression of Christian love.

This is, of course, the best-case scenario. Sadly, it seems there are a sufficient number of times when restoration is not achieved, because Matt 18 and its prescription for achieving reconciliation are not followed. Matthew 18 calls for the offended one to speak privately to the offender and for the offender to acknowledge the pain caused and ask for forgiveness. When no acknowledgment of the offense takes place and no reconciliation is sought, there is an absolute ending of the once-called friendship.

There is no doubt about it. It is a painful business. Deep inner lament occurs. Eventually, it is always followed by the inner questioning "How could I have missed this possibility in our friendship?" Jerome may have been correct, but that still doesn't remove the sting of betrayal. Aristotle defines friendship, in part, as one seeking the good for the other.[9] Clearly, betrayal betrays itself in friendship by seeking harm for the other.

Nevertheless, ending a friendship, no matter how justified, is still one of the most serious actions of one's life. Cicero in his writing *On the Good Life* advocates Cato's caution when he says it is best, if possible, for the friendship to be concluded with "a gradual unstitch[ing] of the union [rather] than to tear it apart."[10] "For if a man has been your friend, it is the most discreditable thing in the world to let him become your enemy."[11] Thus, if a friendship is ended, ways should be sought to "make it clear that what has happened is just a termination of friendship and not a declaration of war."[12]

However, if one has genuinely loved the once-upon-a-time friend, as life continues on and inner healing begins to take place, and often after prayer, one may begin to recall with some pleasure and affection that person who, for a time, brought so much companionship and joy, and even help to your life. Those tender remembrances are part of the process as well and are signs of the healing power of the Holy Spirit and the seeking of the wounded Christian soul. Can one, even after a complete loss of ongoing relationship, still love a former friend? Can one continue on, remembering the good of that person and finding one's heart eased in the pain of loss?

9. Aristotle, *Nicomachean Ethics*, bk. 8, 10.147.

10. Cicero, *On the Good Life*, 215.

11. Cicero, *On the Good Life*, 214.

12. Cicero, *On the Good Life*, 215.

Yes. It is God at work in the seeking soul. True, companionship with the other is no longer trusted or sought. That would be unwise. Still, neither is harm for the other desired. In fact, it is possible to hope and pray for that person to find inner personal restoration, joy, and happiness in their life. Finding that emerging in your life is the sign of the forgiveness of seventy times seven. It is the praying for one's enemies, to use extreme language, that Jesus commands. It is the triumph of love.

Once, in the midst of a personal healing from a friend's betrayal, after much lamenting, I was browsing my library for a book I needed for a lecture and I came across a book of poems that I had received as a birthday present from a dear, but distant, across-the-country soul friend. I must have been busy when I received it, for I shelved it and forgot about it. I casually opened it for a quick browsing. There on the opened pages before me was this wonderful poem. It was a beautiful blessing to me, verifying my emerging feelings, and verifying again the truth of Aelred's writings, first quoting Prov 17:17: "He that is a friend, loves at all times" and continuing with his own comment: "If the one whom you love offends you, continue to love despite the hurt. His conduct may compel the withdrawal of friendship, but never of love."[13]

Perhaps you have come across this book yourself. It's entitled *To Bless the Space between Us*, by John O'Donohue, and includes the poem "For Lost Friends."[14] I recommend it to you if you find a need to work through a personal lament for lost friends. As I read and reread this poem, I found it helpful to remember that Jesus our Lord, who fully knowing his imminent betrayal was at hand and with his own lament welling up in his heart, washed the feet of Judas, the betrayer, as a loving demonstration of the extraordinary grace of God (John 13:1–30).

13. Aelred of Rievaulx, *Spiritual Friendship*, 102.

14. O'Donohue, *To Bless the Space*, 176–77.

9

Friendship and Happiness

IT WAS JUST A few months ago at this writing. It was the blustery, cold month of February in Illinois. The birthday celebration was for our four-year-old granddaughter, a gregarious one. She had been celebrating all day, but that did not seem to have dampened her enthusiasm factor. Her mother, my daughter, has this delightful custom of decorating the dining table the night before the children awake on their birthdays. When the children emerge from their bedrooms, they are confronted with a dining table and chandelier festooned with brightly colored decorations. On a side chair, presents are piled high. All this is to say that to my daughter's credit, the birthday day always begins on a high point. So, by evening, my granddaughter was no stranger to celebration.

The birthday girl and her family arrived at our home after dinner to have ice cream cake and, yes, grandparents' presents. I had hung a happy-birthday banner across the mantle, and there were flowers on the table. A few presents were placed at the fireplace hearth. Our granddaughter arrived excited with anticipation, her long, luscious ginger curls bouncing along with her usual bright, loquacious manner.

The thing that struck me the most was her absolute unbounded joy expressed at the opening of a gift. It went something like this: "Oh, I *love* this! I have *always* wanted this!" We were all delighted as well, delighted with her. I have to admit, Grandpa and I were feeling pretty satisfied with ourselves. Then, came the birthday cards. (It's just too hard to open cards before presents, as we all know.) There among the stack of cards was a card from Aunt Karen, my closest friend, whom the children call "aunt."

My granddaughter opened the card—ripped the card open, I should say. Her mother made a valiant attempt to remind her of who Aunt Karen was and began to read the front of the card. However, the reading was just too agonizingly long for my granddaughter. Unable to wait one more millisecond, my granddaughter flung open the card and four colorful stickers fell out, a sticker for each year. Stickers floated across the family room in a seemingly slow-motion flutter. "I have stickers," my granddaughter shrieked as if she had just won the jackpot. Her eyes widened, her hands raised up in the thrill of it all, her feet left the floor in joyous bouncing. Need I say that this was a successful evening? Our granddaughter went home that night with a smile as big as Chicago. She had become an heiress of stickers! The thrill was absolutely palpable.

After they left, I turned to my husband. "Does anyone have to ask what happiness looks like after this?" We both laughed.

As it turns out, this sort of happiness isn't just the property of four-year-olds. Having reached the age and stage of grandmotherhood and having raised three children of my own, I have other memories. I especially remember my older son's sixteenth birthday party or my ten-year-old son's sleepover birthday party that kept my husband busy all night, playing basketball, baking cookies! I have to smile when I remember my husband's decade birthday with fifty neighbors and friends from our church making it a real delight.

Now what do four-year-old happiness, ten-year-old happiness, sixteen-year-old happiness, and a grandfather's happiness have in common? Meaningful human connection, family and friends. Human nature has us wired to experience the greatest happiness through relationship. From the youngest of us to the oldest, we are naturally created to reach out to others, and to experience happiness because of our connection with others. Epicurus maintained (in modern language): "Of all the things that wisdom provides for living one's entire life in happiness, the greatest by far is the possession of friendship."[1]

Here's a little example that happened just yesterday. On Thursdays of this year's schedule, I take care of my little grandson, who is nearing a year and a half. We were having lunch. A little bit of peanut butter and jelly on a piece of raisin toast, some Yoplait vanilla yogurt, which he insisted upon

---

1. Rubin, *Happiness Project*, 141.

eating with his own spoon (no issue with the dropped globs on the bib), and blueberries, which he loves. His mother asks me to put the food on his high chair tray and let him feed himself, and I've been pretty dutiful in following her directions. So, while he was enjoying his favorite—blueberries—I teased him by making a little smacking sound with my lips and walking my fingers across the tray toward one particular blueberry. This is standard teasing, and he knows it about me. I fully expected him to protect his precious blueberries, but what happened surprised me. I took one of the blueberries in my fingers, and he reached and took it away from me. I expected that. Then, he took the blueberry securely in his small hand and lifted it up to my mouth. I opened my mouth, and he popped it in! Then, he took another blueberry and offered it to me. This time I ate it a bit reluctantly, as that was not the purpose of my teasing. The next blueberry he offered, I said to him, "Oh no, honey, that's your blueberry," but he insisted on holding it up. So, I let him feed me. He smiled. He was happy. He was aware, even at that young age, that there is happiness in connection with others.

This possibility of experiencing happiness in human connection has no income level, no educational requirements, no national identity, and it is immune to age and stage. Happiness because of connection to others is available to every soul on earth. Life in a community and personal connection to a few friends, it turns out, is a lifesaver and a happiness generator.

There's a possibility, if you're like me, that you're wondering about what I've just written in regards to the universal availability of happiness. I would have been hesitant to make such a claim even a few years ago, but since then all sorts of research have emerged that are pretty illuminating. Even worldwide research shows that people all over the world, from the richest to the poorest of countries, identify themselves as basically happy 75 percent of the time. Still, here we sit in the wealthiest nation in the world, and in fact, in all of history, and we wonder about that. We want to ask: You mean people who are spending their days primarily just getting food for the next day, those people are 75 percent of the time identifying themselves as happy? The answer is yes, and here is why. As it turns out, the greatest indicators of potential happiness are family and friends, not money, not even education. Of course, these things can go a long way toward increasing a standard of living, which, with the right choices, can lead to the potential for greater happiness. That is not in dispute.

So, can this mean that a four-year-old living at a poverty level but with shelter, food, and love who receives a small doll for her birthday with a cupcake and a candle can experience the same level of happiness as my four-year-old granddaughter did in February? The surprising answer is yes, if she is safely surrounded by a loving friends and family. With those elements in place, a small doll, a cupcake with a candle, for that little girl, could be happiness itself.

Now, I confess, in certain ways, I almost don't want that to be true. I don't want any of us for one minute to neglect the plight of the poor, to not care about social justice issues, to not have concern for the immigrant, the jobless, the homeless, the addict, the hopeless, the friendless, the lost souls around us. Indifference in this area is never acceptable for a Christian. My point in drawing this similarity is to say that God, in God's good creation, created within all of us a capacity to be enwrapped in that ephemeral ribbon of intense joy we call happiness.

We make a mistake when we attribute happiness as too insubstantial to be a meaningful aspect of life. Some actually minimize the possibility of experiencing happiness when they are no longer young. They make the mistake of attributing sheer, blissful happiness only to the young or the naïve. Happiness in its pure state is available to every soul God created. It is a human capacity. Happiness isn't just the property of children or teens or even grandmothers. Happiness is in the reach of every human being of every age and stage in every place on earth. It is a life option for every individual.

According to Aristotle, "Happiness is the meaning and the purpose of life, the whole aim and end of human existence."[2] Now, as a Christian, I have to take issue with Aristotle, even though I understand happiness to be intrinsic to a good life. Scripture would tell us that the goal of life is to be conformed to the image of Christ. The goal is not purely inner peace. Still here is where we can trip ourselves up. We can understand this conformity to that image to be a dreary, lip-biting, stolid, joyless journey as we each pick up the challenges of our particular personal lives, but that would be a mistake. From the account of creation itself, Scripture tells us that God created the world good, and although that creation has been fractured by sin and yearns for redemption and restoration, there still is much of that goodness that remains. We forget that to our peril. God did not send his Son, Jesus, to discourage our lives but rather to give us hope. When hope is present, happiness is not far behind.

2. Rubin, *Happiness Project*, 14.

It's true that many have debated the distinction between happiness and joy. For the sake of this reflection, I believe that yes, the first flush of happiness can be and usually is the result of a particular event or experience, for example, a happy birthday moment or a new friend. However, Scripture tells us that the joy of the Lord is our strength. This is understood as the deep assurance that our lives are centered in Christ. This is foundational. Yet, as we can see, happiness and joy overlap and can influence each other. The happiness of a wedding and the love it proclaims can result in a joy that transcends all of daily life. So, happiness can flow into deep joy.

I saw an example of deep joy at church recently. It was during the ceremony of awarding third grade Bibles. That Sunday morning third graders were invited up front. Some were eager and others were shy, but they all gathered as was expected. It was a good bunch of children up front! "You are now old enough to read the Bible," the children's minister said in his lilting Australian accent. "This Bible is your very own Bible to read on your own." My third grade granddaughter was thrilled beyond expression. With a big smile, clutching her Bible in her arms, she made her way back to our pew. She had her very own Bible! She was over the moon with excitement. She was careful eating anything after church. She didn't want to smudge her cherished Bible with the sweet icing of the customary donut hole. That night she placed her Bible on the dresser beside her bed. I imagine that even after lights were out, she peeked at the Bible to be sure it was still there. She understood, even as a child, that this Bible was a treasure. This joy she experienced caused me to remember when someone gave me a Bible. I was in my early twenties. I still have it. I cherish it. I read it right away, and after that, my life changed, filled with joy! Even as I remember it, I feel that deep happiness and joy.

Happiness, it turns out, has some very positive companions. Regular strong social interaction and a few very good friends are the highest indicators—not only of happiness, but of longevity. Social connections and good friends are the top two in a list of ten identifying longevity characteristics. The most important factors for long life turn out to be relational, and those are the most important factors for happiness as well. Over and over again, in all sorts of studies, it comes out the same. Let me put it this way: close family and friendship, a few good strong loving friendships, and a wide circle of other friends and even associates are statistically related to personal happiness and long life.

Gretchen Rubin in her book *The Happiness Project* writes: "The most important element to happiness is social bonds."[3] "Everyone from Seneca to Martin Seligman [a positive psychologist superstar] agrees that friendship is the key to happiness."[4] Surprisingly, even Epicurus, the ancient Greek philosopher whose name is popularly associated with pleasure-seeking, even hedonism, maintained that "of all the things that wisdom provides for living one's entire life in happiness, the greatest by far is the possession of friendship."[5]

Now, what if, as you've been reading this chapter, you are convinced that friendship is a source of happiness, and happiness is one of the most important aspects of life? What if you decide (wisely) that you want to be more active and deliberate in friendship? Then, let's continue in this vein to see what can be discovered about this sort of effort.

As Girl Scouts we learned a song that I can still sing today at the drop of a hat! Maybe you know it. The lyrics go like this:

> Make new friends
> But keep the old,
> One is silver
> And the other, gold.[6]

We sang it around the campfire. We sang it at our troop meetings. We sang it in unison, and we sang it in rounds. It is a happy song with a lyrical and easy melody. We sang it with a perky beat. I wonder if any of us ever really thought about what we were singing. Whether we understood it or not when we were ten or twelve years old, it is clear as a bell to me now. Making new friends and keeping the old (longtime) friends is a key to a happy and satisfying life. However, in our very mobile society, many of us don't do that very well at all.

So, let's start with what it means to make new friends.

As a child, if your parents moved for whatever reason, it placed you in the position of starting over, finding new friends. Now, I know, some people just move down the street or around the block, but a whole bunch of us kids moved from state to state, school to school. This is especially true of military brats who often went from a base in one country to a base in

---

3. Rubin, *Happiness Project*, 9.

4. Rubin, *Happiness Project*, 8.

5. Rubin, *Happiness Project*, 8.

6. The lyrics of this old song are attributed to a poem written by Joseph Parry (1841–1903).

another country. Maybe this happened to you: You were loving where you were living, you were loving your school, your church, and your neighborhood playmates. It was your yard where the neighborhood kids came to play softball. You had friends. Then, the move. If you can detect that I am writing about this upheaval from personal experience, you are correct. I moved from city to city, state to state. My father was a corporate executive, and that is what corporate families did, especially in the fifties, sixties, and seventies. Some of the military families I have met moved every year. Their children were in eight or ten or even twelve different schools growing up. If you've lived in pretty much the same place your whole life, this scenario is hard to envision, but it is a real aspect of American life. Whether you were a child or an adult, you were starting over in more ways than just a new home or apartment in a new location. You were starting over relationally.

An important book, *The Organization Man*, written by William H. Whyte and published in 1956, became one of the most influential books published in the last half of the twentieth century. It arrived on an American scene recovering from World War II in a flush of prosperity. It was a time of joy and relief and renewed hopes for family happiness. Soldiers had returned from the military to their hometowns, to their home communities, to their local colleges and universities on the GI bill. After surviving the Great Depression and living through two wars, America was embracing life and faith with gusto. Whyte exposed what many considered to be a shocking reality that was taking place in our culture right under our noses. Three large organizations in our society—the military, the church, and corporate America—were fostering the regular relocation of their people, with one of the goals being that the people's ties to the organization and their friends within the organization would become more crucial to their lives than those friends outside of the organization. The policy was to foster loyalty to the organization. Whyte maintained that in actuality America was changing. The average American was subscribing to an organization's collectivist ethic rather than to rugged individualism. The book *The Organization Man* literally rocked the world, challenging Americans' beliefs about themselves as rugged individualists. It had tremendous implications for matters of friendship and happiness for those within and without those organizations.

According to the Pew Charitable Trust of 2015, historically about 17 percent of American families move in a given year. In a lifetime a person in the US is expected to move 11.4 times. Today, twenty-somethings are moving more.

Of course, people move for a lot of reasons—to be close to family, to keep or to take a job, because they can now afford a better living situation, or even in difficulty, divorce, bankruptcy, and eviction. Whatever the reason, each move involves a complicated relational and logistical maze that must be traversed. Usually everything changes, house and perhaps city, school, church, doctors, pharmacies, grocery stores, neighborhood, and the simple logistics of where does one get this item or that one? Who are insurance agents and repair services that can be trusted? What about a hair salon or a barber shop, as well as a myriad of other aspects not even mentioned here because the list would be too long. Sometimes there is help from others and sometimes not.

My mother, who was a veteran at this, had a rule. She would brook no talk about wishing we were back at our former home. "No," she would say, "our home is here. Wherever we are as a family is where our home is." Now that I look back on this, I realize that that was a good rule. The message was, be positive. Get acquainted. Make friends. The upshot of this is that we did just that. This new city was home, and that was the end of it.

What are guidelines that can be trusted in the midst of making new friends in a new location?

School-age children and working adults have the advantage of being immediately introduced to a school or a work population, but nonetheless, the following guidelines hold for those who want new friends and are willing to seek them.

1. The first guideline is: You're not in Kansas anymore, Dorothy. In meeting new people, remember, they are much less interested in how much you miss your former home. They are much more interested in what you find great about your new location.

2. Look for ways to join and participate in groups who are engaged in your own interests. For example, if you're a singer, a good place to consider is a church choir or a civic chorale. If you love to cook, check out the local stores that offer cooking classes. You'll enjoy it, and you'll meet others who also love to cook. If you love the symphony, join the Symphony Guild.

3. Keep your spiritual roots strong and nourished. As soon as possible, find a church. Some people like to move to a city and church-shop

for a year or two. My observation is what they find is that no church is perfect, and because they don't attend any particular one regularly, even after two years, they hardly know anyone. "The people in the churches here are just not that friendly," they report to their friends in their previous city. Gradually, church hoppers become more and more disengaged. This has the additional unfortunate aspect of causing them little by little to become spiritually disengaged. It weakens their life at a time when they need spiritual strength.

4. Whatever group or organization you associate with, show up, and keep showing up. It can take several months for people there to even recognize you. Then, seemingly suddenly, people recognize you, speak to you, and include you. The key here is to not be discouraged in the months that you are feeling like a part of the furniture. It's normal. Not personal.

5. Try to recognize faces and remember names of those you meet. Pay attention to people whom you like, and keep paying attention to them. If you feel a connection, there's a chance they do too. It's okay to invite someone like this to coffee. Don't make it too much or too long. Keep reaching out. Some of these ones will turn out to be your closest friends in your new location, but it takes time to discern.

6. Don't expect things to move too fast. Remember, everyone in this community probably had a pretty satisfying life before you were even there. Respect that. Inclusion is a slow process, and people have to be convinced that you are sincere and committed to the community or organization.

7. Don't gossip or even talk about others. Keep confidences. Respect your new location. Respect your new relationships. Be a good neighbor. Be kind. Be grateful to God for these new folks in your life.

8. Choose happiness. Researchers have high praise for the natural characteristics of happy people. People like them better. Some of that is because they're friendly and interested in others. They smile. They make better friends, colleagues, and citizens.[7] Choosing happiness has a great benefit in finding and keeping friends.

What about making new friends when one has lived in a community for ages? As it turns out, these guidelines hold even if you've lived in a

7. Rubin, *Happiness Project*, 70.

community for a significant amount of time. The challenge for you is to be open and willing to making new friends. Pay special attention when an existing friend suggests you meet someone your existing friend is especially appreciating. Research shows that there is a higher probability of a new person becoming a friend if that new person is introduced to you by an existing friend. Making new friends can be a challenge, because you already have your circle of friends, and your life and your time are full of them. The key is to be aware of the people God brings into your life. Be alert to those who are potential friends. Try to make an effort to connect with at least one new person a year. Even one new relationship of meaning in your life each year or couple of years will enrich your life tremendously.

"Make new friends, but keep the old," the song goes.

A longtime friend is a treasure beyond measure. However, somehow there is a temptation to take those "old" friends for granted and to assume they will always be there, or to assume they will understand if they don't hear from you. Time and distance, a new city or a new job or a new family member, can contribute to a gradual unintentional disengagement. Suddenly, one turns around, and the friendship is essentially stale, less and less interesting because of less and less time in contact, closer and closer to closure. These closures are usually not abrupt. They just whimper out and reach the Christmas-card-only phase. This is a very real issue for modern people today. Time intrudes its narrowing power on all of us. Everyone, it seems, no matter who they are, will tell you they are "so busy." And the fact is, they generally are.

There are old friendships, of course, that are local, and the possibilities to get together are seemingly endless, but somehow, it just doesn't happen anymore. Maybe your interests have changed, and the things you used to do together just aren't that important to you anymore. Even though you have no ill will towards that old friend, and no conscious effort is being made to avoid them, getting together just doesn't happen. No initiative is taken by either of you, and that seems to be acceptable on both sides. Of course, sometimes, friends change so much that there is little common ground of interest, or there is a deeply eroded foundational trust because of something that has been said or done that violates the friendship. Pastors have a tried-and-true saying: As people get older, they either get bitter or better. Sad but true, some get bitter. After a while, one simply distances oneself.

A friendship in which you have spent considerable time over some years will generally hold when distance and time intrude. Still, it has to be emphasized that it will hold if there are some continued times together, some communication, and some ongoing participation in one another's life, i.e., texts, birthday cards, phone conversations, even only one or two in a year. Nevertheless, for a friendship like this to maintain its resiliency, there had to have been in the past a great number of face-to-face hours spent together. There had to have been a deep bonding. For example, as I have noted before, in my twenties I was in a small group Bible study that met every Friday night for two years. Following the conclusion of that group, the majority of those friends remained close friends. I am no longer in my twenties, and I probably speak to a few of them only once a year, but I still could call them with anything—at any time at all—and I know without a doubt, they would be there for me. Three of them have remained very close throughout all this time.

Finally, on the topic of keeping "old" friends, I consider foundational principles that go a long way to keeping a firm foundation with friends.

First, popular Christian writer, James Martin, maintains an important one. "Give people the benefit of the doubt."[8] I would add, *Assume the best about everyone, and especially your friends.* More often than not, you will discover that you are right.

Second, learn how to forgive, overlook, refuse to harbor grudges, let things go—whatever suits your personal inclination. Nothing, you may say. Try to think again. I would encourage you to find a soft spot in your temperament and apply it regularly to your friend. As we all know, people make mistakes. Sometimes a friend in the presence of others may thoughtlessly make a regrettable statement about you that is subsequently reported to you. Sometimes a friend seems too busy right then to talk on the phone when you really need to talk. Sometimes a friend just doesn't live up to your expectations. It happens. Ask yourself, is this a regular occurrence or something that has happened once or seldom in your friendship? It's always best to talk to your friend about this as soon as possible, but do it in a spirit of understanding and love. Even with the closest of friends there are aspects of their life that are not shared between you—there are hurts in life that are not known to you, there are wounds of life that can never be known without hurting or betraying another person, perhaps another friend. Life is complicated. Friendship is complicated. We all need to learn how to forgive.

---

8. Martin, *Jesuit Guide*, 234.

In conclusion, let me emphasize that God created us to share life with one another. Love your neighbor as yourself, the Scripture teaches. We know that these relationships produce personal happiness and societal good. We also know that happiness in relationship is a strong contributing factor to longevity. It seems that one has to conclude that happiness is very important—and not only for today, or for this month, or this season, or this particular place. Happiness is important for life, and friendship is the key to happiness.

Is it too much to maintain that God wants you to be happy, happy in life and love, and happy in your faith? Oh, that's going too far, some might say. Perhaps, but when I think about the astonishingly beautiful creation in which we live, or the joy of falling in love, or the deep delight in watching your child take her first steps, or the thrill of artistic accomplishment, or the joy of looking around your dinner table with loved ones seated in every chair, or the joy of receiving your very own Bible in the third grade, when I think of all of it, how can we conclude anything else? God, who is full of love and beauty and joy, wants you to experience that joy and the daily experience of happiness. Friendship is one of the key elements that produces happiness in this life and joy in the next. There is no doubt about it.

10

Friendship

Forever

THIS TENTH AND FINAL chapter seems incomplete if I do not share with you a story of a journey I made into a past that is still present today in the here and now.

This journey is what I had considered, in truth, a research trip, but it turned out to be far more than that. You can probably guess that I am inviting you to join me as I travel to a site in northern England called Rievaulx and the monastery of the same name just outside of York. There, we will see the actual place where one man, a Christian abbot by the name of Aelred, made that remote area of northern England noted for Christian friendship and love. As it turned out, visiting there on July 16, 2016, was far more than a research trip. It was one of the great days of my life. I invite you to come along with me.

The day dawned on July 15, 2016, the day of our journey north. John and I drove to York from Cambridge, where we were staying for a few weeks in a comfortable English house with an adjoining English garden of hedges and paths adorned with overhanging tree branches and flowers. John had rented a bright blue sedan that made me laugh at its boldness. "Bright enough?" I teased him when I saw the car.

"We're going on a bold adventure," he explained with cheery bravado and accompanying gestures. It was an adventure indeed!

Driving north or driving anywhere at any distance on the British island requires some serious attention for American drivers, since the Brits drive on the left side of the road. In addition, it always seems to be a mixture of the express highways and village roads dotted with roundabouts where one goes around about in a circle until the road leading in the direction you want to go appears. If you miss your desired road, and it is easy to do, you just go roundabout again. The actual trip from Cambridge to York was measured at 155 miles, as we Americans measure it, and it was mostly on the A1 highway. Still, 155 miles in the UK is not like traveling 155 miles in the US. All in all, we took about four hours to make the trip, arriving in York late afternoon at the Royal York Hotel in time for high tea.

Since we were very hungry at that late afternoon hour, we elected to "take tea," as they say there, and skip dinner. The tea was elegant and delicious. We were not disappointed! Afterwards we explored York, taking in the grand cathedral as well as the central city statue commemorating Constantine the Great who had been crowned Roman emperor there in AD 306. To our surprise and delight we came across the famous Betty's Tea House, as well as a restaurant named Bennett's directly across the street from the cathedral. Bennett's had an unforgettable sign: "We have five loaves and two fishes, as well as roast duck in one of our dishes!" We weren't hungry after tea, but if we had been, we'd have headed right into Bennett's. I am still wondering if the whole menu is in verse. After lingering near the cathedral for a view in the twilight, we headed back to our room. Tomorrow was the Big Day.

So it was on July 16, 2016, after a light breakfast you could see us on the road in a car that was such a bright color that it could be easily viewed from space! If you could have composed a melody of our conversation it would have been light and lyrical, extending throughout the distance from York to Rievaulx, all twenty-six miles.

Finally, we were almost there. Driving on the Rievaulx Bank Road down towards the river and the North York Moors National Park where Rievaulx Abbey is located, I could hardly contain my excitement. As it turns out, the Abbey is protected by the National Park System. Happily, it is designated as a National Heritage Site. "Of course," I commented to John, "It is a national treasure." With the weather cooperating perfectly, it could not have been a more beautiful day. The sky was clear blue—not a single cloud. The sun was shining. The temperature was accommodating, not too hot or humid. Imagine a perfect July day in your own experience, breathe it in and feel the sun on your face, and join us now as we gain our first glimpse of Rievaulx.

Going down into the valley that Aelred himself had described as much like heaven on earth as he could imagine, one can immediately feel the pervading peace of the place. Breathe in the clean, pure air that is almost intoxicating, hear the sound of the River Rye flowing through the valley, look around at the surrounding green hills, and let your eyes fall upon your first view of the ancient abbey. I must confess that the first thing I saw as we drove into the valley was unexpected. "Look!" I laughed to John. There in full view, grazing on the slope of the valley, was a flock of sheep. It was charming to see. I knew that long ago the abbey had partially supported itself by raising sheep and selling the wool; still to see it continuing here after a thousand years was something I hadn't expected. As it turns out, sheep are still being raised and the wool shorn and woven into blankets for sale in the abbey. At the close of the day, I just couldn't resist. I bought a wool blanket to remind me that the blessings of Rievaulx and the blessings of God continue today. But I am getting ahead of my story.

As I raised my eyes from beyond the flock of sheep and gazed deep into the valley, I saw the old ruins of the abbey. It was much grander, much larger, with many more buildings than I had expected. The vaulted arches of the great church drew my eyes to heaven as they must have for those worshipping a millennium before. While there was evidence of multiple structures, some were reduced to their foundations. Still others stood at varying heights. Many of those walls remained erect at the place where loving hands had borne them from nearby quarried hills and gently placed them over a thousand years before. They remained, those stout walls, although all of the roofs had long since collapsed or burned.

Walking among the ruins of the buildings, it seemed impossible not to consider how all this could have begun here—here in this remote valley that requires a traveler to actively search to find it—here where a thousand years later, pilgrims are still coming. As it turns out, it was quite a story.

You may remember that it was during the first millennium that the Roman Empire gradually collapsed. Rome withdrew its forces from England in the fifth century, making way for the Saxons and the Angles as well as the Vikings to raid England until finally in 1066 William the Conqueror, a Norman, established his rule. In the meantime, Rome moved its forces closer to Rome itself until, eventually, barbarian pagan tribes overran Europe, rampaging, looting, burning, destroying cities, and making slaves of the people. It was a time of real fear among the population and, we know now, a massive transition to a new order. Some sought to defend against barbarian paganism by establishing small communities of monks who would preserve the faith of the Church. Thus, new Christian religious orders were founded. Each order sought to create guidelines or a "rule" for its community to organize its life together. The most popular was St. Benedict's Rule, a guide to living a life in balance, a life of virtue and goodness and true happiness. Essentially the monks spent about five hours a day in prayer services. This was termed the *opus Dei*, the work of God. In addition, the monks worked with their hands to support the monastery and provide aid to the surrounding community. *Ora et labora*, pray and work, was the rule.

Okay, but what about Aelred, you may ask? You remember that Aelred, a young man attached to the court of King David of Scotland, was living a life enviable to many. He was successful and popular at court, but something was deeply unsettling to him in his soul. His writing confirmed that he felt an emptiness with court life, an interior restlessness. As a Christian of deep faith, raised by a father and grandfather both married priests, he struggled with whether life at court was really what God wanted for him. Knowing this provides us with a more complete appreciation of Aelred's response to God's call to dedicate his life to God at Rievaulx. Looking back, we can see that God was preparing Aelred for the moment when he discovered Rievaulx. For us today, we are reminded of Thomas Merton, another Christian of world renown, who struggled with similar inner struggles before he first visited the Abbey of Gethsemani in Kentucky. Aelred heard the call of God, and he responded with his whole heart and his whole life. As it turned out, Aelred's decision to commit his life to God at Rievaulx not only changed Aelred's life but had a profound effect on Christians the world over.

Having thoroughly explored the ruins of the abbey, aided by a diagram in an available pamphlet, we were able to gain a more complete mental image of the abbey and its place in the valley. Each of the buildings' ruins was identified. However, there was one small construction that John had difficulty locating in the pamphlet. We were stumped! "Oh, I see it now," John said, excitedly pointing to the diagram. "It's the warming house."

"The what?" I asked, thinking that I had not heard him correctly.

"It's the warming house," he repeated and read, "This is where the monks could go to warm themselves. The large fireplace was lit on All Saints Day and remained burning until the warm weather returned."

"Well, that solves that mystery," I said and then added, "I vote for central heating!" We both laughed.

Tired from climbing amid the ruins of the abbey, we headed into the floor of the valley where we were surprised again when we saw up front for ourselves all sorts of life going on. There were a multitude of people there. Men, women, boys, and girls were dressed in the costumes of the abbey period. Small tents were erected with pennant-type borders. Children were playing and laughing. Toddlers were toddling. Musicians were playing as they walked among the crowd. Food was being prepared on outdoor grills, and other food was being sold. It was as alive a community of joy and celebration as any Fourth of July celebration in our hometown of Wheaton, Illinois, where we sit in our folding chairs on the sidewalk of our church and watch our neighbors parading by, with marching bands playing and makeshift floats on the back of pickup trucks, while clowns are throwing candy and children scrambling for it. There was no doubt. Life was still going on at Rievaulx Abbey!

"Well, this is lively, just look!" John smiled.

Yes, look, I thought, all of this life still expressing itself. All this since AD 1132—an entire millennium ago. I tried to imagine the genesis of all this. I had read that Bernard of Clairvaux sent twelve monks to Rievaulx to found a sister Cisterian monastery. Today we would say that it was something like church planting where one congregation sends some of its leaders to begin or "plant" a congregation in another location. William of Malmesbury was to be their leader, the first abbot in this great endeavor. The truth is that when they arrived, they discovered a beautiful valley, of course, but it was hard going to carve a living space suitable for them in the densely wooded area. It wasn't exactly heaven on earth. Lest one have an overly romantic idea of all this, the first year they very nearly starved to death.

Aelred came to Rievaulx when it was already established, although primitively. Some years passed before Aelred became the third abbot from AD 1147 to 1167, which under his leadership became the time of its peak of prominence. It was under Aelred's leadership that the majority of the buildings comprising the beautiful complex were built, and it was under Aelred's preaching and teaching that the community grew in number to its largest size. At its peak, Rievaulx Abbey was a community of six hundred and forty men, which was comprised of one hundred and forty monks and five hundred lay brothers who lived and worked with the monks and often did the heaviest labor. In fact, during Aelred's time of leadership at Rievaulx, Aelred was the most prominent religious figure in all of England, as well as an advisor to the king of England, Henry II, and in demand as a conciliator, historian, and biblical expositor. The name of Rievaulx was known in the courts of England, Scotland, France, and the papal court in Rome. When the abbey was forcibly closed, it was a particularly great loss because the abbey was renowned as a significant spiritual center beyond its borders and had been one of the most important sites of Christian religious life in all of England and the world.

By the time it was late afternoon, we decided to visit the newly constructed welcome center, where there was a rest area, a tiny shop, and a small, bright, little cafeteria serving sandwiches, drinks, and sweets. We took our drinks out onto the freshly laid patio where there were patio tables and chairs. "It's been perfect," I said to my husband, referring to our day. "All I could have hoped for and more," I said.

"Me too," he replied almost in a hush as he looked thoughtfully at the community fair. "Look what an emphasis on Christian friendship has done through the ages," he said.

"Yes, look!" I replied as much to him as myself.

So what did Aelred teach about friendship that was so extraordinary, you may be thinking? Not surprisingly, that was the topic of our drive back to York after a day at Rievaulx. Of course, just before we got into our car, we each turned around to cast one long lasting look at this place that had been the site of extraordinary blessing for so many. As we drove south towards York, we rehearsed the day to one another, back and forth with free-flowing thoughts and smiles. Then, after a bit of a pause, John said, "So what was it that Aelred taught about friendship that changed how Christians understood friendship?"

With a question like that and a captive audience of my husband driving, how could I resist? "There are few significant teachings about the living of a good life more important than Aelred's teaching," I said, and I began with considerable enthusiasm.

"That's quite an intro," John said with a chuckle in his voice. "I think I had better prepare myself for a thorough explanation that will last, oh, I imagine, about the length of our trip back to York."

"I wouldn't want to disappoint you," I teased back, and with that, we were off.

"Aelred believed that friendship was a significant part of life's goodness. He believed that Christian spiritual friendship begins in Christ, continues in Christ, and is perfected in Christ. He defined friendship as 'mutual harmony in affairs human and divine coupled with benevolence and charity.'[1] But his shorter definition was 'two friends together with Christ as their bond.'

"At one point he wrote, and I memorized this, it's so important: 'I call them more beasts than men who say that life should be led that they need not console anyone.'[2] As I just said, he considered that real friendship was defined as two friends and Christ. He emphasized over and over again that human beings need one another, and we all need friends in Christ. At one point he echoed Cicero, illustrating that if you had everything and no one to share it with, having everything would not bring any pleasure. You would wither without human companionship."

"I see that," John said. "After all, where would I be without you and all your ideas?" he joked.

"Not at Rievaulx!" I couldn't help but tease back.

I continued, "Don't misunderstand. Aelred was not naïve. He understood that human relationships differ considerably. Not everyone can or would want to be that committed to Christ and someone else. Even among those who are committed to Christ, the truth is that everyone cannot be a close friend. Aelred delineated general human relationships as falling into three categories: carnal, worldly, spiritual. According to him, carnal friendships begin in sharing similar vices. Worldly friendships begin in a hope of gain from the other. Spiritual friendships begin with a similarity of life and morals and seek the just (or the good).[3] Cicero, from whom Aelred takes his basic definition of friendship, believed that next to goodness, friendship was the highest relationship to which anyone could aspire.

"Aelred is distinctive because he believed that because we were made in the image of God, it was possible for us to be friends with God. He understood Christian friendship as a relationship with three parties, the two friends with Christ as their bond. When close friends in Christ relate in such a way that they each encourage the other to be all that Christ calls them to be, spiritual growth, spiritual formation takes place in each of them. Aelred understood that these sorts of relationships are not numerous in anyone's life. They are rare in the scope of any one life. Most people can manage only a very few, perhaps a handful, of these relationships, because they require a mutual affection, mutual trust, and a mutual commitment to Christ. In short, spiritual friendships take time. If you think about it, when

1. Aelred of Rievaulx, *Spiritual Friendship*, 53, referencing Cicero.
2. Aelred of Rievaulx, *Spiritual Friendship*, 17.
3. Aelred of Rievaulx, *Spiritual Friendship*, 59.

you are in a Christian spiritual friendship and you find yourself tempted with a hint of jealousy of the other, it is important for you to refuse to indulge that feeling, to reject that temptation with Christ's help. Or if you find that you are tempted to do or say something against your friend in Christ, again you must reject that temptation with Christ's help."

"That sounds like only the perfect are able to have that sort of friendship," John observed.

"Not the perfect," I said, "but those who really love their friend and are committed to the friendship. Of course, forgiveness is an element in human friendships. Aelred realized that evil is present in all of us as part of fallen humanity. Nevertheless, if one friend loves the other, temptation becomes possible to overcome. Christian spiritual friendship highlights those elements that express love of Christ and the friend, as well as the fruits of the Spirit. When this expression of pure love in friendship is mutually evidenced, that is spiritual friendship. Aelred maintains that spiritual friendship is eternal. Spiritual friendship continues on into eternity, into heaven. You may be surprised by this, but this was not a unique aspect of Christian theology in the early centuries. Somehow over the ages, this affirmation of the eternal nature of Christian spiritual friendship faded away. Yet, if you turn back to St. Augustine's writings you would find him writing that Christian spiritual friendships are eternal; 'In Christ friendships are eternal and death brings no permanent loss.'"[4]

"You have mentioned this before to me," John said. "Remember that time when you said that because we are friends in life and both of us committed to Christ, we would be with one another in heaven?"

"Yes, that's what I was saying. Jesus said there was no marriage in heaven, but we know the Lord valued love and human friendship. Certainly in heaven, it's not about sexual expression; it's about faithful love expressed from the heart. That's how it would be."

I continued, "Aelred embraced John 15:15 where Jesus tells his disciples that he no longer calls them servants but friends. Later Jesus tells them in that same evening that he would not eat of the bread or drink of the wine until he ate with them in the kingdom [Matt 26:29]. Jesus clearly expects to share in friendship with them in heaven. Aelred is credited with reasserting the truth that friendships in Christ continue with Christ into eternity."

John was quiet. "It makes me think of Don and Hugo," he said. "They were dear friends in Christ."

4. Carmichael, *Friendship*, 61.

"Yes," I said, "they were. Someday you will be with them again. Aelred would say that our friendships in Christ never end."

John nodded. "You know, I have to say that it changes the way I look at friends and friendship. It makes me realize that Christ was in it in the beginning. It was in Christ that we met, and we continued in Christ. We prayed together and supported one another with our companionship and care. So that friendship in Christ continues and will continue." His voice trailed off a bit . . . thinking.

"Yes," I agreed. "One could say that it was Christ himself who sends us those friends who love him, and it is up to us to embrace those friendships or not. Much of it has to do with how we listen to the Holy Spirit whispering into our lives."

"It makes me wonder, though, what about people who don't have spiritual friendships?" John said.

"I know. It's sad to think about. The thing about friendship that is so glorious is that it is never too late in life to make a friend or revive a friendship. There is no age limit to having friendships, no expiration date either. Spiritual friendships are available to every human being if they are willing to love Christ and another as Christ commanded. Potential spiritual friends are all around us, everywhere in our churches—and possibly even in our own families, our own neighborhoods, our friends we met in school. In making friends, the important thing for everyone is to get started!"

By the time we had finished discussing Aelred and spiritual friendship, our journey was completed. We returned to our hotel and settled in for the night. The next day, we would retrace our steps back to Cambridge feeling somehow changed and refreshed after such a close experience of Rievaulx. Nevertheless, our minds continued to consider the joyful expectation of precious friends continuing with us into eternity. Somehow it seemed as if heaven were all around us.

In the first chapter of this book, I began by telling you that I think about heaven a lot. Perhaps you will join me in considering that those Christians whom you have loved and cared for are now in heaven. They have made a great journey, a journey into eternity. In closing, join me in a thinking of what it would be like to be there yourself.

Imagine it! It is a place beyond this place. A place brimming with eternity, heaven. Think of your great joy. There before you are all glory and radiance, music of unimaginable beauty, rarified space vibrating with the power of love—all beauty that had seemed impossible, possible—and all that was beyond imagining, imagined, all that you thought indescribable, describable. In the midst you hear the singing of angels, and worship that is a very part of the atmosphere. Around you are the ones whom it had seemed were gone in your life, found. Family who had been grievously absent, present. Precious friends whom it had seemed were lost to your life, found. There are the great ones of the faith from the past, the cloud of witnesses, present. Now those of the distant ages, face to face. For this is fulfilled reality, as it was always intended to be, and joyously, thrillingly, there is the Lord who now abides with humanity.

More than this we cannot go in this present, for we are limited by our capacity to see beyond this life. Nevertheless, we have hints in Scripture of a new heaven and a new earth as well as our own life in the Spirit who reassures us in hope. Perhaps this will imbue your thoughts, as it does mine, with the joy of a heavenly future.

I think about heaven a lot. Now perhaps you will too. Much joy is ahead!

St. Augustine is said to have written these words. May they bless you.

> Alleluia.
> All shall be Amen and Alleluia.
> We shall rest and we shall see.
> We shall see and we shall know.
> We shall know and we shall love.
> Behold our end which is no end.[5]

5. Augustine, as quoted in Tutu, *African Prayer Book*, xx.

Bibliography

Aelred of Rievaulx. *Spiritual Friendship*. Translated by Mary Eugenia Laker. Kalamazoo, MI: Cistercian, 1977.

Aristotle. *Nicomachean Ethics*. Translated by Joe Sachs. Focus Philosophical Library. Newburyport, MA: Focus, 2002.

Bakhtin, M. M. "Discourse in the Novel." In *The Dialogic Imagination: Four Essays*, edited by Michael Holquist, translated by Caryl Emerson and Michael Holquist, 259–421. Austin: University of Texas Press, 1981.

Barth, Karl, and Carl Zuckmayer. *A Late Friendship: The Letters of Karl Barth and Carl Zuckmayer*. Grand Rapids: Eerdmans, 1982.

Benner, David. *The Gift of Being Yourself*. Downers Grove, IL: InterVarsity, 2004.

Bonhoeffer, Dietrich. *Life Together*. Translated by John W. Doberstein. New York: Harper, 1954.

Buber, Martin. *I and Thou*. Translated by Ronald Gregor Smith. 2nd ed. New York: Scribner's, 1958.

Carmichael, E. D. H. *Friendship: Interpreting Christian Love*. London: T&T Clark, 2004.

Cicero. *De Amicitia*. In *Cicero: On Old Age, On Friendship, On Divination*, translated by W. A. Falconer, Loeb Classical Library 154, 103–213. Cambridge, MA: Harvard University Press, 1923.

———. *On the Good Life*. Translated by Michael Grant. London: Penguin, 1971.

Dillard, Annie. *The Writing Life*. New York: Harper Perennial, 1990.

Gottman, John M., and Nan Silver. *The Seven Principles for Making Marriage Work*. New York: Harmony, 1999.

LaCugna, Catherine Mowry. "God in Communion with Us: The Trinity." In *Freeing Theology: The Essentials of Theology in Feminist Perspective*, edited by Catherine Mowry LaCugna, 83–114. San Francisco: HarperSanFrancisco, 1993.

Lawrence, Brother, and Frank Laubach. *Practicing His Presence*. Library of Spiritual Classics 1. Sargent, GA: Seed Sowers, 1973.

Lewis, C. S. *The Four Loves*. New York: Harcourt Brace Jovanovich, 1960.

Martin, James. *The Jesuit Guide to (Almost) Everything*. New York: HarperCollins, 2010.

Munger, Robert Boyd. *My Heart—Christ's Home*. Rev. ed. Downers Grove, IL: InterVarsity, 1986.

O'Donohue, John. *To Bless the Space between Us: A Book of Blessings*. New York: Doubleday, 2008.

Peterson, Jordan. *12 Rules for Life*. Toronto: Random House Canada, 2018.

Powell, Pamela Baker. "Friendship: The Lost Spiritual Discipline." In *Tending Soul, Mind, and Body: The Art and Science of Spiritual Formation*, edited by Gerald L. Hiestand and Todd Wilson, Center for Pastor Theologians Series, 134–44. Downers Grove, IL: IVP Academic, 2019.

Rohr, Richard. *Falling Upward: A Spirituality for the Two Halves of Life*. San Francisco: Jossey-Bass, 2011.

Rubin, Gretchen. *The Happiness Project*. New York: HarperCollins, 2009.

Sartre, John Paul. *No Exit: A Play in One Act*. Adapted from the French by Paul Bowles. New York: French, 1958.

Tutu, Desmond. *An African Prayer Book*. New York: Doubleday, 1995.

Wadell, Paul J. *Friendship and the Moral Life*. Notre Dame, IN: University of Notre Dame Press, 1989.

Whyte, William H., Jr. *The Organization Man*. New York: Simon & Schuster, 1956.